THE GREAT TREKS OF THE ALPS

Trekking the Tour des Combins

by Andrew McCluggage

KNIFE EDGE Outdoor Guidebooks

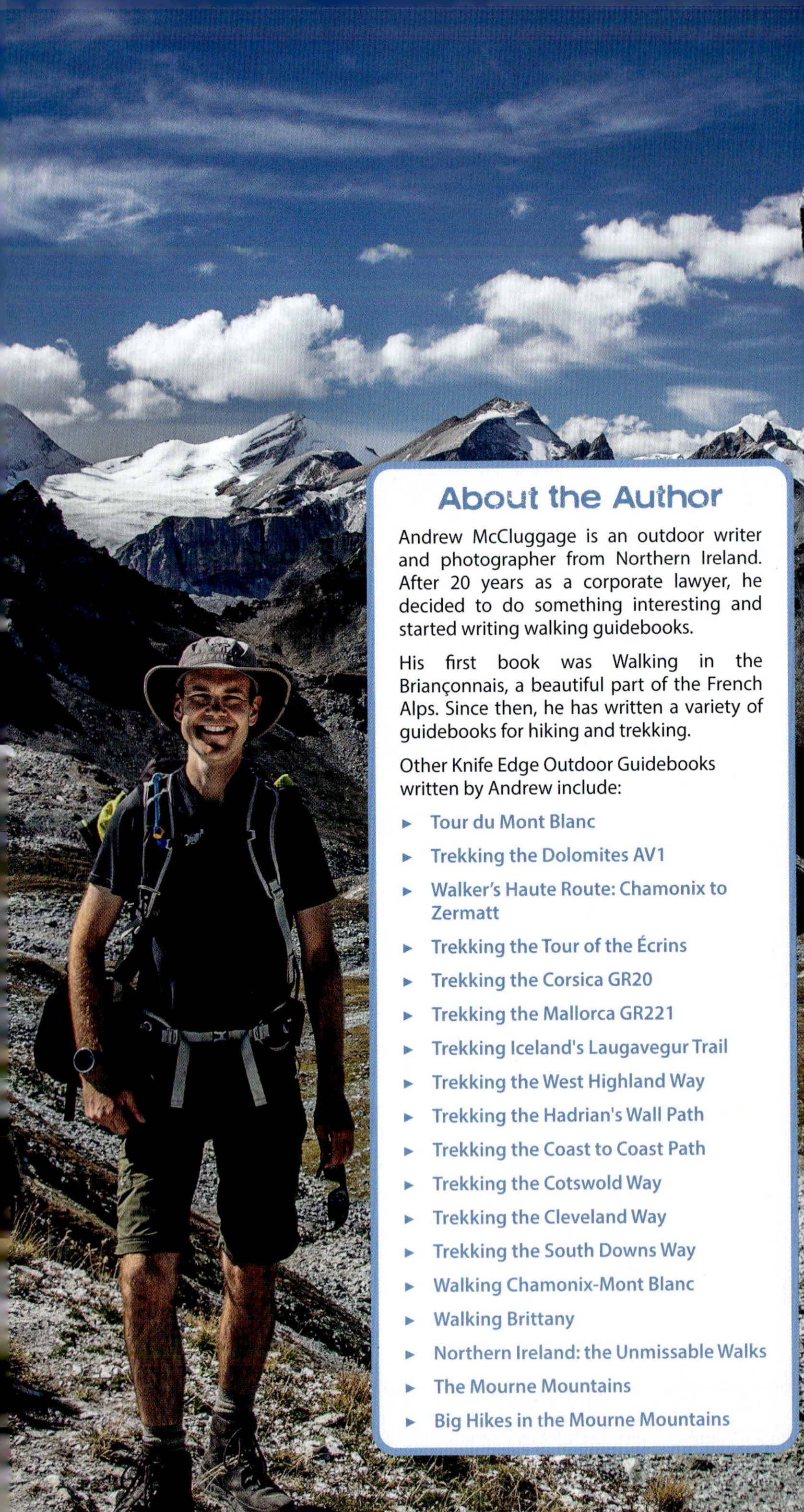

About the Author

Andrew McCluggage is an outdoor writer and photographer from Northern Ireland. After 20 years as a corporate lawyer, he decided to do something interesting and started writing walking guidebooks.

His first book was Walking in the Briançonnais, a beautiful part of the French Alps. Since then, he has written a variety of guidebooks for hiking and trekking.

Other Knife Edge Outdoor Guidebooks written by Andrew include:

- Tour du Mont Blanc
- Trekking the Dolomites AV1
- Walker's Haute Route: Chamonix to Zermatt
- Trekking the Tour of the Écrins
- Trekking the Corsica GR20
- Trekking the Mallorca GR221
- Trekking Iceland's Laugavegur Trail
- Trekking the West Highland Way
- Trekking the Hadrian's Wall Path
- Trekking the Coast to Coast Path
- Trekking the Cotswold Way
- Trekking the Cleveland Way
- Trekking the South Downs Way
- Walking Chamonix-Mont Blanc
- Walking Brittany
- Northern Ireland: the Unmissable Walks
- The Mourne Mountains
- Big Hikes in the Mourne Mountains

One of the spectacular
Lacs de Fenêtre (Stage v6)

Publisher: Knife Edge Outdoor Limited (NI648568)
12 Torrent Business Centre, Donaghmore, County Tyrone, BT70 3BF, UK
www.knifeedgeoutdoor.com

First edition 2024
ISBN: 978-1-912933-18-1

A catalogue record for this book is available from the British Library.

Front and back covers: Descending towards Mont Vélan (Stage v6)
Title page: Petit Combin & Glacier de Corbassière (Stage 3a)
This page: Sunset view from Cabane de Mille (Stage 1/v1/2a)
Back cover flap: Lac de Mauvoisin (Stage 3b)

All routes described in this book have been recently walked by the author and both the author and publisher have made all reasonable efforts to ensure that all information is as accurate as possible. However, while a printed book remains constant for the life of an edition, things in the countryside often change. Trails are subject to forces outside our control. For example, landslides, tree-falls or other matters can result in damage to paths or route changes; waymarks and signposts may fade or be destroyed by wind, snow or the passage of time; or trails may not be maintained by the relevant authorities. If you notice any discrepancies between the contents of this guide and the facts on the ground, then please let us know. Our contact details are listed at the back of this book.

Contents

Route Descriptions

Stream flowing into Val de Bagnes (Stage 2a)

Getting Help

Emergency services number: dial 112

Distress signal

The signal that you are in distress is 6 blasts on a whistle spaced over a minute, followed by a minute's silence. Then repeat. The acknowledgment that your signal has been received is 3 blasts of a whistle over a minute followed by a minute's silence. At night, flashes of a torch can also be used in the same sequences. Always carry a torch and whistle.

Signalling to a helicopter from the ground

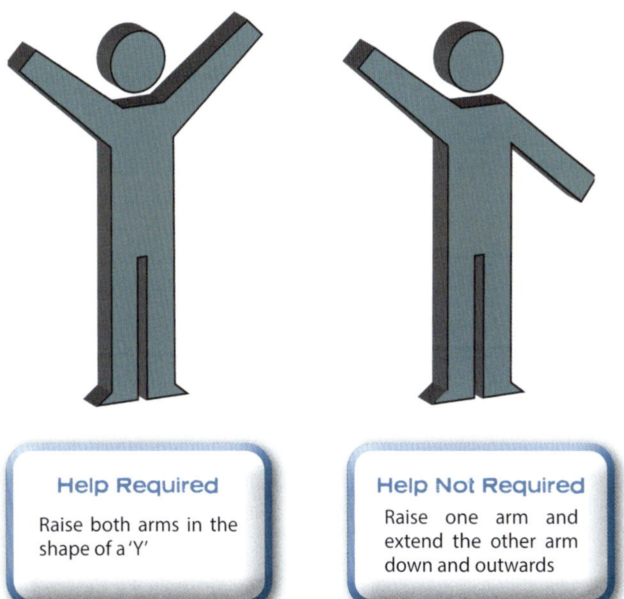

WARNING

Hills, cliffs and mountains can be dangerous places and walking is a potentially dangerous activity. Some of the routes described in this guide cross potentially hazardous terrain. You walk entirely at your own risk. It is solely your responsibility to ensure that you and all members of your group have adequate experience, fitness and equipment. Neither the author nor the publisher accepts any responsibility or liability whatsoever for death, injury, loss, damage or inconvenience resulting from use of this book, participation in the activity of mountain walking or otherwise.

Some land may be privately owned so we cannot guarantee that there is a legal right of entry to the land. Occasionally, routes change as a result of land disputes.

Lac de Mauvoisin (Stage 3b)

Introduction

Grand Combin de Grafeneire (4313m)

In this digital age, social media has a significant influence on our choice of travel destinations. Eye-catching images, shared over and over on the various platforms, tend to funnel travellers towards a handful of 'bucket list' locations while many equally fabulous places are overlooked. And so it is with long-distance treks. The Tour du Mont Blanc (TMB), for example, has attained an exalted status, attracting legions of hikers each year, whereas many other incredible Alpine treks entice relatively few. It is true that the TMB is exceptionally beautiful and deserves its popularity but there are many other equally spectacular treks in the Alps that are unjustifiably and inexplicably undiscovered.

One of these unsung heroes is the relatively new Tour des Combins (TDC), a trek which is, in fact, only one narrow mountain ridge away from the TMB. Just like its more famous contemporary, the TDC circumnavigates a spectacular alpine massif: in this case, the Grand Combins Massif (which is immediately adjacent to the Mont Blanc Massif). Clear paths and tracks lead you along spectacular ridges, across high mountain passes and through spectacular valleys. Day by day, the terrain changes and surprising new landscapes are displayed. There are jagged snow-capped peaks seemingly everywhere, shimmering alpine lakes of turquoise and blue, flower-filled pastures of the deepest green and exhilarating suspension bridges over deep chasms. And if that was not enough, the path traverses the moraine of the incredible Corbassière Glacier which, at 9.8km long, is one of the longest in Europe: you will find yourself as close to a glacier as you can get without actually stepping onto it. Like the Mont Blanc Massif, the GC Massif spans international frontiers and the trek passes through both Switzerland and Italy: the shifts in culture, language and food are highlights of the trek.

For the most part, accommodation takes the form of remote mountain huts: there are five of them and their locations are remote and spectacular; all of them sit above 2100m and four out of the five are located above 2400m; one of them, Cabane FXB Panossière, perches precariously on a promontory on the edge of the Corbassière Glacier. However, on the W side of the massif (between St-Rhémy and Bourg-Saint-Pierre), there are no huts and you will have to make use of hotels or the pilgrims' dormitories in the monastery at Col du Grand-Saint-Bernard (which has been providing refuge to travellers for 1000 years).

Taking all of this into account, it is not surprising that the TDC can give the TMB a run for its money. They are worthy rivals and each has something different to offer. The TMB may have Mont Blanc, the highest mountain in Western Europe, but the TDC has the permanently snow-capped Grand Combin de Grafeneire (which, at 4313m, is itself no minnow) and, in any case, the TDC itself provides fantastic views of Mont Blanc. Furthermore, the TDC boasts some unique features that the TMB does not possess: for example, its proximity to the huge Corbassière Glacier and a stay in a thousand-year-old monastery. Also consider the wildness of the terrain on the TDC's E side where it traverses one of the most remote parts of the Alps: vehicular access is largely restricted by the imposing walls of Mont Blanc de Cheilon. Finally, those seeking tranquillity will be pleased to note that hiking the TDC is a much more peaceful experience than many of the better-known Alpine treks. Although you will share the trail with others, the number of hikers is relatively low, especially along the remote E side of the GC Massif. Although there can be many day-walkers, the vast landscape is easily large enough to swallow them and most do not explore very far from the parking areas in the accessible valleys. Get a reasonably early start and you will find yourself largely alone for much of the day.

In short, the TDC is one of the most unique and rewarding treks in the Alps. There is a clear sense of wilderness and adventure. Those who walk this trail witness wild and spectacular scenery which is accessible to very few. It is Alpine trekking at its best and it will be an experience that you will never forget.

The TDC is 102km (64 miles) long with 6,100m (20,200ft) of ascent/descent. Those statistics may sound intimidating but it is reassuring to note that plenty of normal people complete the trail each year: with the right preparation, planning and approach, it is manageable for most people of reasonable fitness. Yes, it is a challenge but it is an achievable one. And that is where this book comes in: most of what you need to know to plan, and prepare for, the TDC is here within these pages and the entire route is described in detail to guide you on the trail itself. Furthermore, unlike some other books, this one contains real topographical maps: for each stage, there are 1:40,000 scale maps to go with the accurate and concise route descriptions. Because we were unable to find commercially available maps which suited our purposes, we commissioned our own maps which are perfect for navigating the trail. As well as including those maps in this book, we have also published a sheet map for the TDC which is extremely helpful for planning and navigation: '***Trekking Map: Tour des Combins***' (ISBN 9781912933525).

We aim to ensure that you have the best chance possible of completing the trek. We place great importance on the correct preparation and we focus in detail on modern lightweight equipment (see p34). We also believe that it is crucial to match your itinerary to your experience, fitness and ability. Accordingly, we have included here an extraordinary level of detail on itinerary planning: our unique itinerary planner has 10 different itineraries to choose from. For each itinerary, we have completed for you all the difficult calculations of time, distance and altitude gain/loss. This makes it easy for you to design a manageable itinerary that suits your specific needs. Once on the trail, you will be able to relax and fully enjoy one of the world's great treks.

The Grand Combin Massif: basic facts

- The GC Massif is a large glaciated massif, in the Pennine Alps. It is located E of, and immediately adjacent to, the Mont Blanc Massif.
- It contains a host of summits including four which are higher than 4000m: Grand Combin de Grafeneire (4313m), Aiguille du Croissant (4260m), Combin de Valsorey (4184m) and Combin de la Tsessette (4135m).
- The massif straddles the Switzerland/Italy border, however, its highest parts are all located within the Canton of Valais in Switzerland.
- Snow remains on the NW faces of the high summits throughout the year. However, the S and E faces are steeper and free of snow. The snow falling on the summits feeds several glaciers, the largest of which is the 9.8km long Corbassière Glacier.
- Val d'Entremont and Val de Bagnes form the massif's W and E boundaries respectively.
- The first people to reach the summit of Grand Combin were Daniel, Emmanuel and Gaspard Balleys, Charles Sainte-Claire Deville and Basile Dorsaz (30 July 1859).

How hard is the TDC?

The TDC is a multi-day trek with significant distances to travel each day. It crosses remote landscapes of mountains, hills and valleys: each day, you will need to climb and descend significantly to negotiate the undulating terrain. Sometimes, the climbs and descents are steep and challenging. As the days go by, such exertions take their toll on your body, both physically and mentally. Accordingly, a reasonable level of fitness is required and the fitter you are at the start of the trek, the better your chances of success and the more you will enjoy the experience.

The demand on your body is intensified by the requirement to carry a pack. However, because of the huts and hotels along the route, it is not essential to carry camping equipment or food (other than basic rations) and therefore your bag can be kept light. Even so, it is fair to say that many trekkers set off carrying some equipment which is unnecessary or simply too heavy: this can contribute to injury and/or exhaustion, leading to abandonment. Accordingly, you should give equipment choice careful consideration: it will be crucial to your enjoyment of the trek and the likelihood of success.

Sometimes paths are steep, rocky and challenging underfoot. Occasionally, you might have to climb up or down short sections of boulders but fortunately, you will not require any technical scrambling/climbing skills. On occasion, the route is exposed with large drops.

For the most part, the paths/tracks are clear, well-marked and simple to follow in good conditions: only occasionally is the route less obvious and more difficult to follow. Consequently, most people have no major difficulties staying on course. However, take care in poor conditions or low visibility when navigation on the highest sections of the trail can be tricky. Furthermore, on the high points of the trail, snow can remain into July, covering paths and making progress/route-finding more difficult.

Many who have completed the TMB (the most famous Alpine trek) look to the TDC for their next trekking experience. Accordingly, it can be useful to compare these two treks. The TDC is much shorter (102km compared to 174km) and has less climbing (6,100m compared to 9,700m). Accordingly, it is usually completed more quickly than the TMB (6-7 days compared to 10-12 days). On paper therefore the TDC is the easier of the two treks. However, the bare statistics do not tell the full story and there is an additional factor which increases the difficulty of the TDC slightly: the remoteness and high altitude of much of the terrain means that there are fewer facilities along the route of the TDC than you will find on the TMB. Because there are fewer locations where you can spend the night, there are fewer ways to break up the trek to suit your own fitness and experience. Consequently, you are locked into a few fairly long stages. Most of these are comparable in difficulty to those on the TMB, however, Section 4 (between Chanrion and Champillon) is notably harder: because it is 23km long and has no facilities mid-route, it is a tough challenge for some trekkers.

Notwithstanding the challenges, thousands of hikers walk the TDC each year. It is therefore an achievable endeavour. To improve fitness, it is sensible to train in advance: there is no substitute for training hikes, carrying a pack. Although not absolutely necessary, previous experience of trekking will help. And, of course, the level of difficulty depends upon how quickly, and how far, you travel each day: faster itineraries are obviously more challenging than slower ones and the TDC will be more manageable if you choose an itinerary that matches your fitness and experience. Most people walk the TDC in 6-7 days. However, fit and experienced hikers could finish it faster. Others prefer to walk more slowly, allowing 8 or 9 days to soak up all the delights on offer. Our Itinerary Planner will help you decide what is best for you.

The tunnel at Mauvoisin (Stage 3b)

Direction and start/finish points

The TDC is a circuit and accordingly, if you walk the full route, you will return to your starting point at the end of the trek. Traditionally, most trekkers start at Bourg-St-Pierre (BSP) and walk in a clockwise direction. However, because you can hike in either direction, this book caters for both clockwise and anti-clockwise trekkers: full route descriptions and plenty of different itineraries are provided for each approach. Furthermore, the numbered waypoints on the real maps make the route easy to follow in either direction.

For those hiking the official route of the trek (including Stage 6), the question of direction has no easy answer: if we had to choose, we would say that trekking CW is marginally easier because the three hardest sections (3,4 and 5) are probably slightly less challenging when hiked in that direction. However, for those choosing to hike our Stage v6 variant (instead of the official Stage 6), a CW approach is definitely easier because Stage v6 has significantly less climbing in that direction: ACW trekkers attempting Stage v6 face a mammoth climb of more than 1600m which will be too much for some, especially on the first day of the trek. It is also worth bearing in mind that, because most hikers travel CW, that is probably the more sociable approach: you are more likely to bump into the same people each day, making it easier to develop trail friendships.

BSP is the most popular starting point because it is the easiest place along the route of the trek to access by public transport: furthermore, starting at BSP ensures that you do not face the hardest sections of the route until the middle of the trek. However, it is also possible to start from Mauvoisin, St-Rhémy or Col du Grand-St-Bernard. Bear in mind though that Section 4, the toughest part of the trek, needs to be hiked all on the same day: it makes sense to have a few days to warm up before tackling it.

You can also start/finish the trek at Orsières which is a short distance off-route, down the valley, N of BSP: our Stage v1 variant uses a spectacular waymarked path to travel directly between Orsières and Cabane de Mille. This makes it possible for CW trekkers to start the TDC from the train station in Orsières without having to catch a bus to BSP. The downside for CW trekkers is that Stage v1 is significantly harder than Stage 1, with much more climbing. ACW trekkers can also use this route to descend directly from Cabane de Mille to Orsières station, saving a lot of time.

The climb to Cabane FXB Panossière (Stage 2b)

Starting Point	Pros	Cons
Bourg-St-Pierre	Daily bus service from/to Orsières train station **Reasonable selection of places to stay, including a campsite** Time to warm up before Section 4 (the hardest stage) **Car parking** A few bars and restaurants for a victory celebration	Long climb on the first day (in either direction)
Mauvoisin	Daily bus service from/to le Châble train station **Lovely remote setting** More time for ACW trekkers to warm up before Section 4 **Car parking**	Only one place to stay/eat **Little time for CW trekkers to warm up before Section 4** Long climb on the first day (in either direction)
St-Rhémy	Beautiful village **More time for CW trekkers to warm up before Section 4**	No public transport **Only one place to stay/eat** Less time for ACW trekkers to warm up before the tougher stages **Long climb on the first day (in either direction)**
Col du GSB	Daily bus service from/to Orsières train station **Magnificent setting** Monastery/museum to visit Reasonable selection of places to stay More time for CW trekkers to warm up before Section 4 **Car parking**	Less time for ACW trekkers to warm up before the tougher stages **Takes longer to reach from Orsières train station than BSP**
Orsières (OR)	Best access by public transport: trains & buses **No need to catch bus to BSP** Grocery shops **Car parking** Time to warm up before Section 4 (the hardest stage) **Bars/restaurants for a victory celebration**	Very long climb on the first day for CW trekkers: more difficult than starting at BSP **Few places to stay**

Hiking Shorter Sections of the TDC

Walking the TDC in one go is a wonderful experience but there are other ways to enjoy this incredible trail. You could walk some parts of the TDC as day-walks or you could hike to one of the wonderful huts, stay the night and then return the next day. During the hiking season, daily buses serve BSP (Stage 1/6/v6), Mauvoisin (Stage 3a/3b) and Col du GSB (Stage 5b/6/v6): there are day-walks along the TDC from each of these places.

If you only wish to walk some of the highlights of the trek then we would suggest the following options (all of which are served by public transport):

- **Cabane de Mille (1 or 2 days):** hike from BSP/Orsières to Cabane de Mille (Stage 1/v1). Then retrace your steps the same day or the following morning (after a night at the cabane).
- **Cabane de Mille & Cabane Brunet (2 days):** on day 1, hike from BSP/Orsières to Cabane de Mille (Stage 1/v1). Spend the night at Cabane de Mille. On day 2, hike to Cabane Brunet (Stage 2a) and then descend into Val de Bagnes (see p63). From there, you can catch a bus to le Châble train station.
- **Cabane FXB Panossière & Glacier de Corbassière (1 or 2 days):** buses travel between le Châble train station and Mauvoisin. Hike from Mauvoisin to Col des Otanes (Stage 3a) for superb views of the glacier. Then retrace your steps the same day or the following morning (after a night at the nearby Cabane FXB Panossière).
- **Lacs de Fenêtre (1 day):** hike from Col du GSB to Lacs de Fenêtre (Stage v6). Then retrace your steps.

Guided tours, self-guided tours or independent walking?

A frequently asked question is whether to walk independently or with an organised group. The answer is a personal one and depends upon your own particular circumstances and requirements. For many, the decision to organise the trek themselves, and to walk independently, can be almost life-changing, opening the door for other challenges in the future. There is much satisfaction to be gained from planning and navigating a trek yourself and the sense of achievement on completion is to be savoured.

However, the independent trekker usually carries a full pack and is responsible for all daily decisions such as pacing, which way to go at junctions, when to stock up with food and water, and choice of route in bad weather. For some, this will be too great a burden on top of the physical effort required simply to walk the route. For those walkers, a guided group is a great solution: the tour company typically organises food and accommodation and the guide makes all the decisions, enabling the walker to concentrate on the walking. On some treks, tour companies can organise transfer of luggage to your accommodation each night but on the TDC, the remoteness of most of the accommodation means that this is not possible: even guided trekkers need to carry their own packs. There are several tour companies operating guided trips on the TDC but you should check whether they cover the full official route or just some of the highlights.

Self-guided tours are much more popular and are a sensible middle-ground. The tour company books all the accommodation and provides advice and information on walking the route. However, you will walk the trail without a guide. Normally, breakfast and evening meals will be provided and you can request packed lunches. As with guided tours, TDC trekkers on self-guided packages will need to carry their own packs.

In recent years, there has been a rise in the number of businesses offering guided/self-guided tours. Consequently, some of the accommodation along the TDC is block-booked in advance by the tour companies. At peak times, this makes it harder for the independent trekker to secure accommodation unless booked well in advance. As a result, many confident trekkers (who would be perfectly capable of walking independently) book a self-guided trip simply to avail of the accommodation booking service. By booking a tour, much of the hassle of planning the trek is alleviated, albeit at a price.

When to go

The weather window for hiking the TDC is quite short: the trekking season starts towards the end of June and ends around the end of September. Even in this period, high winds, heavy rain, and low cloud (which reduces visibility), can occur: occasionally, it can even snow on the trail. You will probably hike in fine weather but you should prepare for the worst. Throughout the main trekking season, there is plenty of daylight. The relative merits of each season are discussed in detail below but, taking all the factors into consideration, we prefer to hike the TDC in the first two weeks of September.

Late June: this can be the most beautiful time for walking. The weather is often sunny and warm. The peaks are frequently at their most photogenic, still fully frosted with snow. Summer haze has not yet arrived so visibility is generally excellent with wide-ranging views. This is peak season for the wild-flowers. Fewer visitors means that accommodation is easier to find and significantly, the mountains are more peaceful. However, as with all Alpine treks, snow sometimes remains on the high cols until early July, making parts of the route difficult and/or dangerous: in such conditions, crampons/spikes and/or an ice axe might be helpful. There are now some very light, compact crampons available which weigh a mere 300g so carrying them just in case is not the burden it once was.

July/August: this is the main summer season when the high cols are normally passable. During July/August, accommodation is harder to find and advance booking is recommended unless you are camping. It can be hot, reaching more than 30°C. Mornings often start with clear and sunny skies and heat up as the sun gains height. If there is to be cloud or haze, often this will arrive in the afternoon when thunderstorms are more likely. Start walking early in the morning to complete the main climb while the temperature is cooler and before storms arrive.

As July progresses, the trails gradually become busier. The busiest time is probably the first two weeks of August, when many of the Swiss, Italians, and French will be taking annual vacations. Towards the end of August, the number of trekkers starts to decrease.

September: this can be the best month for walking as the weather is often more settled than in summer. Skies are usually clear and visibility excellent. Daytime temperatures are still warm but evenings get cooler and the days get shorter. As the month progresses, the risk of snowfall on the cols increases but any snow usually clears quickly. Visitor numbers gradually reduce: the mountains are quieter and there is less demand for accommodation. However, towards the end of the month, some accommodation starts to close for the season so check availability in advance.

October: this can be a very beautiful time, with spectacular autumn colours. However, careful planning is needed to undertake the route in October. As the month progresses, the possibility of snowfall on the cols increases which could make them impassable or dangerous. Check the weather forecasts carefully along the way to avoid getting trapped by snow between cols. If fresh snow is forecast, do not set out. Some accommodation will be closed. You will need to be prepared to carry more food as there will be fewer places to eat. Trekking in October is for experienced and well-equipped hikers only.

The viewpoint above Col de Mille (Stage 1/v1/2a)

Month	Pros	Cons
Late June	Pleasant temperatures **Frequent sunny skies** Good visibility **Wild flower season** Fewer trekkers **Hut beds easier to find** Longest days	Snow on the high parts of the trail: cols and peaks occasionally inaccessible
July/August	Generally reliably fine weather **High cols normally passable** Long days	The hottest period **Sometimes hazy** Afternoon thunderstorms **Visitor numbers highest** Hut beds harder to find **Some snow remains in early July**
September	Pleasant temperatures **Frequent sunny skies** Excellent visibility **Fewer visitors** Hut beds become easier to find **Autumn colours** Still sufficient daylight	Accommodation closes as the month progresses **Cooler evenings** Increasing possibility of snow
October	Autumn colours **Frequent sunny skies** Excellent visibility **Fewer visitors**	Greater possibility of snow **Much accommodation closed** Short days **Cold mornings and evenings**

Approaching Cabane de Mille (Stage 1)

Using this book

This book is designed to be used by walkers of differing abilities. Many guidebooks for long-distance treks rigidly divide the route into a fixed number of long day-stages, leaving it up to the hiker to break down those stages to design daily routes which suit his/her abilities. This book, however, has been laid out differently to give the trekker flexibility: it divides the route into 9 shorter stages which you can combine to design daily routes that meet your own specific needs.

Each stage covers the distance between one accommodation option and the subsequent one. Every accommodation option on the route is the start/finish point of a stage. You can choose how many of these stages you wish to walk each day. Each stage has its own walk description, route map and elevation profile.

The labelling of the stages uses a combination of numbers and letters. It is a simple system but requires a little bit of explanation. Firstly, we have divided the route into 6 'Sections' (numbered from 1 to 6 in a CW direction): each Section represents one day of our standard 6-day schedule. Within some Sections, the route is further broken down into two stages: these stages are labelled with a number between 1 and 6, representing the relevant Section that the stage is part of. These stages are also labelled with a letter. So, for example, the first stage in Section 3 is 'Stage 3a' and the second stage is 'Stage 3b'. Take a look at the detailed Itinerary Planner below and all should become clear.

The Itinerary Planner includes a range of tables outlining 10 suggested itineraries of 6, 7, 8 and 9 days. We include itineraries for both CW and ACW trekkers. In each table, we have crunched the numbers for you so there is no need for you to waste time (and mental strength) working out daily distances, timings and altitude gain/loss.

Of course, the suggested itineraries are only suggestions. You can shorten or lengthen your day to suit yourself: just decide how many stages you want to walk that day. It is up to you. As there is accommodation at the end of every stage, it is easy to design your own bespoke itinerary and adjust it on the ground as you go (subject to accommodation availability).

For example, day 2 of the standard 6-day itinerary involves walking Stages 2a and 2b. However, you could decide to extend your day by walking Stages 2a, 2b and 3a, all on the same day. Or you might be tired and decide to shorten your day by walking only Stage 2a. With some other guidebooks, you would have to work out how to split stages yourself, involving some complicated maths to plan distances and times going forward. This guide, however, does all the hard mental work for you.

In this book:

Timings indicate the approximate time required by a reasonably fit walker to complete a stage. They do not include stoppage time. Do not get frustrated if your own times do not match ours: everyone walks at different speeds. As you progress through the trek, you will soon learn how your own times compare with those given here and you will adjust your plans accordingly.

Walking distances are given in kilometres (km) to match maps and signposts in Europe. One mile equates to approximately 1.6km.

Place names in brackets in the route descriptions indicate the direction to be followed on signposts. For example, "('Mauvoisin')" would mean that you follow a sign for Mauvoisin.

Ascent/descent numbers are the aggregate of all the altitude gain or loss (measured in feet and metres) on the uphill or downhill sections of a stage. As a rule of thumb, a fit walker climbs 1000 to 1300 feet (300 to 400m) in an hour. The statistics tables in the route descriptions are based on CW itineraries: ACW trekkers should simply swap the ascent and descent figures.

Elevation profiles are provided for each Section, indicating where the climbs and descents fall on the route. The profiles are based on CW itineraries: ACW walkers should simply read them in reverse.

Real maps are provided. These are extracts from 1:40,000 scale maps produced by Knife Edge Outdoor Guidebooks. On the maps, we have marked the route of the trek, the start/finish points of stages, significant waypoints and the accommodation along the TDC. On each map, N is at the top of the page. As well as printing these maps in this book, we have also published a sheet map for the TDC which is extremely helpful for planning and navigation: '***Trekking Map: Tour des Combins***' (ISBN 9781912933525).

The following abbreviations are used:

ACW	Anti-clockwise/counter-clockwise
BCE	Before the Common Era (a secular alternative to 'BC')
BSP	Bourg-St-Pierre
CE	The Common Era (a secular alternative to 'AD')
CW	Clockwise
GC Massif	Massif of the Grand Combin
GSB	Grand-St-Bernard
OR	Off-route
TDC	Tour des Combins
WW1/WW2	World War 1/World War 2
TL	Turn left
TR	Turn right
SH	Straight ahead
N, S, E and W, etc.	North, South, East and West, etc.

The N side of Fenêtre de Durand (Stage 4)

Itinerary Planner

All our itineraries start/finish at BSP. However, if you prefer to begin at Mauvoisin, St-Rhémy or Col du GSB, simply start reading from that location in our tables. If you wish to start/finish at Orsières, simply substitute Stage v1 for Stage 1 (see p54 for Stage v1 statistics). Furthermore, each of the itineraries incorporates the official Stage 6 route. However, in good conditions, we recommend Stage v6, our high-level variant which is scenically superior: simply swap Stage 6 for Stage v6. See p102 for Stage v6 statistics.

Anti-Clockwise

Stage	Start	Finish	Time (hr)	Distance km	Distance miles	Ascent m	Ascent ft	Descent m	Descent ft	Max Alt m	Max Alt ft
6	Bourg-St-Pierre	Col du GSB	5:20	12.1	7.5	1055	3461	206	676	2469	8101
5b	Col du GSB	St-Rhémy	2:15	7.0	4.4	42	138	892	2927	2469	8101
5a	St-Rhémy	Rifugio Champillon	6:15	15.1	9.4	1296	4252	450	1476	2709	8888
4	Rifugio Champillon	Cabane de Chanrion	9:00	23.0	14.3	1199	3934	1203	3947	2797	9177
3b	Cabane de Chanrion	Mauvoisin	4:00	11.6	7.2	369	1211	989	3245	2629	8626
3a	Mauvoisin	Cabane FXB Panossière	4:30	7.3	4.5	1088	3570	288	945	2875	9433
2b	Cabane FXB Panossière	Cabane Brunet	2:30	7.2	4.5	191	627	729	2392	2641	8665
2a	Cabane Brunet	Cabane de Mille	3:45	7.9	4.9	710	2330	340	1116	2473	8114
1	Cabane de Mille	Bourg-St-Pierre	3:45	11.4	7.1	218	715	1071	3514	2560	8399

Clockwise

Stage	Start	Finish	Time (hr)	Distance km	Distance miles	Ascent m	Ascent ft	Descent m	Descent ft	Max Alt m	Max Alt ft
1	Bourg-St-Pierre	Cabane de Mille	5:00	11.4	7.1	1071	3514	218	715	2560	8399
2a	Cabane de Mille	Cabane Brunet	3:00	7.9	4.9	340	1116	710	2330	2473	8114
2b	Cabane Brunet	Cabane FXB Panossière	3:30	7.2	4.5	729	2392	191	627	2641	8665
3a	Cabane FXB Panossière	Mauvoisin	3:00	7.3	4.5	288	945	1088	3570	2875	9433
3b	Mauvoisin	Cabane de Chanrion	5:00	11.6	7.2	989	3245	369	1211	2629	8626
4	Cabane de Chanrion	Rifugio Champillon	9:00	23.0	14.3	1203	3947	1199	3934	2797	9177
5a	Rifugio Champillon	St-Rhémy	4:45	15.1	9.4	450	1476	1296	4252	2709	8888
5b	St-Rhémy	Col du GSB	3:15	7.0	4.4	892	2927	42	138	2469	8101
6	Col du GSB	Bourg-St-Pierre	3:40	12.1	7.5	206	676	1055	3461	2469	8101

Suggested Itineraries: Clockwise

BSP is the most popular starting point and therefore all our CW itineraries start with the long climb from BSP to Cabane de Mille. Those who begin at Mauvoisin and St-Rhémy will also have long climbs on the first day. For an easier first day, you could start at Col du GSB: day 1 would then involve the largely downhill Stage 6 to BSP.

6 Days: the classic TDC itinerary is popular because it enables many European trekkers to fit the trek (including travel) into a one-week vacation slot. However, it is a demanding itinerary with more than 1000m of climbing every day except day 6. Furthermore, days 3, 4 and 5 are particularly challenging, each with more than 1200m of climbing/descent. Some trekkers may prefer to split one or more of the longest days by choosing one of our slower itineraries.

Day	Stages	Time (hr)	Distance		Ascent		Descent	
			km	miles	m	ft	m	ft
1	1	5:00	11.4	7.1	1071	3514	218	715
2	2a, 2b	6:30	15.1	9.4	1069	3507	901	2956
3	3a, 3b	8:00	18.9	11.7	1277	4190	1457	4780
4	4	9:00	23.0	14.3	1203	3947	1199	3934
5	5a, 5b	8:00	22.1	13.7	1342	4403	1338	4390
6	6	3:40	12.1	7.5	206	676	1055	3461

7 Days Option A: identical to the classic 6-day itinerary except that the tough Section 3 (between Cabane FXB Panossière and Cabane de Chanrion) is split into two days with an overnight stop in the hotel at Mauvoisin. This gives you two easier days before the challenging Section 4.

Day	Stages	Time (hr)	Distance		Ascent		Descent	
			km	miles	m	ft	m	ft
1	1	5:00	11.4	7.1	1071	3514	218	715
2	2a, 2b	6:30	15.1	9.4	1069	3507	901	2956
3	3a	3:00	7.3	4.5	288	945	1088	3570
4	3b	5:00	11.6	7.2	989	3245	369	1211
5	4	9:00	23.0	14.3	1203	3947	1199	3934
6	5a, 5b	8:00	22.1	13.7	1342	4403	1338	4390
7	6	3:40	12.1	7.5	206	676	1055	3461

The descent into Italy from Fenêtre de Durand (Stage 4)

7 Days Option B: identical to the classic 6-day itinerary except that Section 5 (between Rifugio Champillon and Col du GSB) is split into two days with an overnight stop in the village of St-Rhémy. This means that you undertake the long climb to Col du GSB at the start of the day rather than at the end.

Day	Stages	Time (hr)	Distance		Ascent		Descent	
			km	miles	m	ft	m	ft
1	1	5:00	11.4	7.1	1071	3514	218	715
2	2a, 2b	6:30	15.1	9.4	1069	3507	901	2956
3	3a, 3b	8:00	18.9	11.7	1277	4190	1457	4780
4	4	9:00	23.0	14.3	1203	3947	1199	3934
5	5a	4:45	15.1	9.4	450	1476	1296	4252
6	5b	3:15	7.0	4.4	892	2927	42	138
7	6	3:40	12.1	7.5	206	676	1055	3461

8 Days: significantly easier than the classic 6-day itinerary. Section 3 (between Cabane FXB Panossière and Cabane de Chanrion) and Section 5 (between Rifugio Champillon and Col du Grand-St-Bernard) are each split into two days. Day 5 is the hardest and helpfully, it sits within the second half of the trek.

Day	Stages	Time (hr)	Distance		Ascent		Descent	
			km	miles	m	ft	m	ft
1	1	5:00	11.4	7.1	1071	3514	218	715
2	2a, 2b	6:30	15.1	9.4	1069	3507	901	2956
3	3a	3:00	7.3	4.5	288	945	1088	3570
4	3b	5:00	11.6	7.2	989	3245	369	1211
5	4	9:00	23.0	14.3	1203	3947	1199	3934
6	5a	4:45	15.1	9.4	450	1476	1296	4252
7	5b	3:15	7.0	4.4	892	2927	42	138
8	6	3:40	12.1	7.5	206	676	1055	3461

9 Days: this is our easiest itinerary. It is identical to the 8-day itinerary except that Section 2 (between Cabane de Mille and Cabane FXB Panossière) is also split into two days with an overnight stop at Cabane Brunet. Day 6 is the hardest and helpfully, it sits within the second half of the trek.

Day	Stages	Time (hr)	Distance		Ascent		Descent	
			km	miles	m	ft	m	ft
1	1	5:00	11.4	7.1	1071	3514	218	715
2	2a	3:00	7.9	4.9	340	1116	710	2330
3	2b	3:30	7.2	4.5	729	2392	191	627
4	3a	3:00	7.3	4.5	288	945	1088	3570
5	3b	5:00	11.6	7.2	989	3245	369	1211
6	4	9:00	23.0	14.3	1203	3947	1199	3934
7	5a	4:45	15.1	9.4	450	1476	1296	4252
8	5b	3:15	7.0	4.4	892	2927	42	138
9	6	3:40	12.1	7.5	206	676	1055	3461

Suggested Itineraries: Anti-clockwise

Hiking ACW is slightly tougher than going CW. Wherever you start, you will be faced with a long climb on the first day: the only solution to this is to begin the trek at Col du GSB and spend the first night at St-Rhémy. However, that would make your first day very short and therefore this option does not appeal to many hikers.

An ACW itinerary is less suitable for trekkers who are planning to hike Stage v6 because it is significantly harder in this direction. Furthermore, ACW trekkers starting at BSP would face Stage v6 on the first day which would be a tough introduction to the trek.

6 Days: our base ACW itinerary is popular because it enables many European trekkers to fit the trek (including travel) into a one-week vacation slot. However, it is a demanding itinerary with plenty of climbing every day, except day 6. Furthermore, days 2, 3 and 4 are particularly challenging with at least 1200m of climbing/descent each day. Some trekkers may prefer to split one or more of the longest days by choosing one of our slower itineraries.

Day	Stages	Time (hr)	Distance		Ascent		Descent	
			km	miles	m	ft	m	ft
1	6	5:20	12.1	7.5	1055	3461	206	676
2	5b, 5a	8:30	22.1	13.7	1338	4390	1342	4403
3	4	9:00	23.0	14.3	1199	3934	1203	3947
4	3b, 3a	8:30	18.9	11.8	1457	4780	1277	4190
5	2b, 2a	6:15	15.1	9.4	901	2956	1069	3507
6	1	3:45	11.4	7.1	218	715	1071	3514

7 Days Option A: identical to the classic 6-day itinerary except that the tough Section 3 (between Cabane de Chanrion and Cabane FXB Panossière) is split into two days with an overnight stop in the hotel at Mauvoisin.

Day	Stages	Time (hr)	Distance		Ascent		Descent	
			km	miles	m	ft	m	ft
1	6	5:20	12.1	7.5	1055	3461	206	676
2	5b, 5a	8:30	22.1	13.7	1338	4390	1342	4403
3	4	9:00	23.0	14.3	1199	3934	1203	3947
4	3b	4:00	11.6	7.2	369	1211	989	3245
5	3a	4:30	7.3	4.6	1088	3570	288	945
6	2b, 2a	6:15	15.1	9.4	901	2956	1069	3507
7	1	3:45	11.4	7.1	218	715	1071	3514

Sunset lighting up Grand Combin (Stage 1/v1/2a)

7 Days Option B: similar to the 7-day Option A itinerary except that days 1 and 2 are structured differently. On the first day, you will not stop overnight at Col du GSB. Instead, you continue down to the village of St-Rhémy to spend the first night. This means that you undertake the long climb to Rifugio Champillon at the start of the following day rather than in the heat of the afternoon.

Day	Stages	Time (hr)	Distance km	Distance miles	Ascent m	Ascent ft	Descent m	Descent ft
1	6, 5b	7:35	19.1	11.9	1097	3599	1098	3603
2	5a	6:15	15.1	9.4	1296	4252	450	1476
3	4	9:00	23.0	14.3	1199	3934	1203	3947
4	3b	4:00	11.6	7.2	369	1211	989	3245
5	3a	4:30	7.3	4.6	1088	3570	288	945
6	2b, 2a	6:15	15.1	9.4	901	2956	1069	3507
7	1	3:45	11.4	7.1	218	715	1071	3514

8 Days: significantly easier than the classic 6-day itinerary. Section 5 (between Col du GSB and Rifugio Champillon) and Section 3 (between Cabane de Chanrion and Cabane FXB Panossière) are each split into two days. Day 4 is still very hard but there is no way around that.

Day	Stages	Time (hr)	Distance km	Distance miles	Ascent m	Ascent ft	Descent m	Descent ft
1	6	5:20	12.1	7.5	1055	3461	206	676
2	5b	2:15	7.0	4.4	42	138	892	2927
3	5a	6:15	15.1	9.4	1296	4252	450	1476
4	4	9:00	23.0	14.3	1199	3934	1203	3947
5	3b	4:00	11.6	7.2	369	1211	989	3245
6	3a	4:30	7.3	4.6	1088	3570	288	945
7	2b, 2a	6:15	15.1	9.4	901	2956	1069	3507
8	1	3:45	11.4	7.1	218	715	1071	3514

9 Days: this is our easiest itinerary. It is identical to the 8-day itinerary except that Section 2 (between Cabane FXB Panossière and Cabane de Mille) is also split into two days with an overnight stop at Cabane Brunet. Day 4 is still very hard but there is no way around that.

Day	Stages	Time (hr)	Distance km	Distance miles	Ascent m	Ascent ft	Descent m	Descent ft
1	6	5:20	12.1	7.5	1055	3461	206	676
2	5b	2:15	7.0	4.4	42	138	892	2927
3	5a	6:15	15.1	9.4	1296	4252	450	1476
4	4	9:00	23.0	14.3	1199	3934	1203	3947
5	3b	4:00	11.6	7.2	369	1211	989	3245
6	3a	4:30	7.3	4.6	1088	3570	288	945
7	2b	2:30	7.2	4.5	191	627	729	2392
8	2a	3:45	7.9	4.9	710	2330	340	1116
9	1	3:45	11.4	7.1	218	715	1071	3514

Accommodation

Rifugio Champillon (Stage 4/5a)

Due to the remote nature of the terrain, the route of the TDC only passes through a handful of tiny settlements: BSP, Mauvoisin, St-Rhémy and Col du GSB. Although there are a few different places to stay at BSP and Col du GSB, each of Mauvoisin and St-Rhémy has only one accommodation option. Away from these settlements, the only accommodation along the trail is in five mountain huts in five different locations. In summary, accommodation along the trail is fairly limited and it is wise to book ahead especially during the busy summer period. In June and September, fewer people walk the route and available accommodation may be easier to find: however, we still recommend that you book in advance because, in most places, there are no alternatives if the accommodation is already full when you arrive. Also bear in mind that before mid-June, and after the third week of September, some accommodation may be closed.

All accommodation is numbered and marked on the maps in this book. Detailed accommodation listings are provided on pages 21 and 22. All contact details were correct at the date of press but this information frequently changes: please let us know about any changes you notice.

Hotels: the majority of hotels are in the one to three star categories and quality varies. Normally, they offer 'half-board' (bed, breakfast and dinner) which can be good value. Most hotels have their own websites.

Chambres d'hôte/B&Bs: simple bed and breakfast accommodation. Normally, you will have a private room with an ensuite bathroom.

Cabanes/Refuges/Rifugi: these are mountain huts which offer dormitory accommodation, meals and drinks (including alcohol). On the TDC, it is rarely possible to book a private room in mountain huts. The huts are situated in the heart of the mountains where they are accessible only to hikers: the settings are spectacular. A stay in a hut can be one of the highlights of a mountain adventure such as the TDC. Although prices have risen in recent years, the huts are still good value: see p28. Dormitories are mixed-sex. Mattresses, pillows and duvets/blankets are provided but you will need a sleeping sheet: this is a thin bag made of silk/cotton which can be purchased cheaply at most outdoor shops. There are usually facilities for charging electronic devices but you may have to queue.

The opening/closing dates for each hut are different and change from year to year. Usually, they open sometime in June and close sometime in September/October. Each hut's website usually sets out the season's opening/closing dates. You can book the huts online (using their individual websites), except for Rifugio Champillon (which is booked by phone/email). Cabane de Chanrion is a Club Alpin Suisse (CAS) hut and offers a discount to members of alpine clubs. For mountain hut etiquette, see p20.

Camping

Cabane FXB Panossière (Stage 2b/3a)

The only campsite along the route of the TDC is at BSP, the most common start/finish point of the trek. Otherwise, the campsite that is most useful to TDC trekkers is located OR at Bonatchiesse, 1.7km N of Mauvoisin (Stage 3a/3b). There are also campsites OR at Champsec in Switzerland and Valpelline and Étroubles in Italy, however, they are all a long walk downhill from the trail.

The rules on wild camping (bivouacking) on the TDC are complicated. The trek enters two countries and different rules apply in each. Irrespective of the rules, emergency bivouacking (where you have no choice due to injury, exhaustion, etc.) is usually tolerated and is unlikely to be penalised. Wherever you pitch up, ensure that you leave no trace: for wild camping guidelines, see p20.

Switzerland: under Article 699 of the Swiss Civil Code, forests, pastures and meadows are accessible by everyone. It does not prohibit wild camping, however, it does state that this general access right is subject to any specific restrictions imposed by a competent authority in the interests of conservation: accordingly, local authorities in the relevant canton/municipality can override Article 699. Putting it simply, the general rule is that wild camping is permitted unless it has been expressly prohibited/limited by another more specific law which has been implemented locally.

In the parts of Switzerland crossed by the TDC, there is one such specific law which limits the general rule: wild camping is expressly prohibited in certain protected areas including hunting ban reserves, designated wildlife protection areas and nature reserves. This means that you are not permitted to wild camp in any parts of the TDC which lie within these types of areas. You can see the extent of these areas on a map at **www.map.geo.admin.ch**, however, the web page is incredibly difficult to use: you must select from various data options so that the map displays only the information that you need. Fortunately, the Swiss Alpine Club has done the hard work for you and displays the map (with the correct filters applied) on its own website: **www.sac-cas.ch/de/umwelt/bergsport-und-umwelt/campieren-und-biwakieren**. The map shows that the following places along the TDC are reserves/protection areas where wild camping is not permitted:

- **Stages 1/v1:** large sections of the TDC route. However, the restriction does not cover the zone around Col de Mille
- **Stage 2a:** the forest of le Mortay which is on the N side of the TDC route between Col de Mille and (1)

- **Stage 3a:** between Col des Otanes and Mauvoisin
- **Stage 3b:** between Mauvoisin and Mont Rouge. This means that wild camping is prohibited along the northern two-thirds of Lac de Mauvoisin (on its E side only).
- **Stage 6/v6:** between ③ and ④

If you are intending to wild camp in Switzerland, you should check this map carefully to make sure that you will be camping outside of the relevant prohibited areas.

Italy: the Italian parts of the TDC are located in the Aosta Valley where wild camping is only permitted above 2500m and only between sunset and sunrise. Only small portions of the route in Italy lie above 2500m: above Col du GSB and around Fenêtre de Durand and Col de Champillon.

Wild camping guidelines:

- **Leave no trace:** you should leave the environment in exactly the same condition as you found it. Leave nothing behind and take nothing away with you. When you have packed up and are ready to leave, look back on your campsite and make sure that another person would not be able to tell that you have been there (except for the flattened grass where your tent was pitched).
- **Do not light open fires:** climate change is upon us and bush-fires are becoming more common. Parts of the trail are close to wooded areas so the lighting of open fires carries risk. Do not be that person who accidentally destroys acres of pristine countryside.
- **Perform toilet duties responsibly:** this means that you should use a trowel to dig a hole in which to 'do your business'. There are some incredibly lightweight backpacking trowels available these days. Your hole should be at least 30m from water-courses. Fill the hole in afterwards and carry away your used toilet paper in a bag that you have brought along specifically for that purpose. Defecating and placing a stone on top is not acceptable: animals can move stones and imagine how you would feel if you sat down next to such a place! Also carry out tampons and sanitary towels.
- **Be discreet and have respect for others:** try to camp where others cannot see you. Keep your group small: it is supposed to be a 'wild' experience. Do not make a lot of noise at night.
- **Stay for only one night** at a particular spot and then move on.
- **Pitch up late and break camp early:** it is good practice to pitch up after 7pm and break camp before 7am.

Mountain hut etiquette

- On arrival, check in at the warden's office.
- Take off your boots and wet clothing at the front door and store them in the places provided at the entrance.
- Do not make noise after 10pm as most walkers go to bed early.
- If you change your plans, cancel your reservation as soon as possible to allow someone else to take your place.

Accommodation Listings

Stage		Name	Facilities	Contact Details
1 Bourg-St-Pierre	1	Hotel Bivouac Napoleon		+41 (0)27 787 11 62 info@bivouac.ch www.bivouac.ch
1 Bourg-St-Pierre	2	Hotel du Crêt		+41 (0)27 787 11 43 reception@hotel-du-cret.ch www.hotel-du-cret.ch
1 Bourg-St-Pierre	3	Camping Grand Saint Bernard		+41 (0)79 370 98 22 reservation@campinggrand-st-bernard.ch www.campinggrand-st-bernard.ch
1 Bourg-St-Pierre	4	Auberge les Charmettes		+41 (0)27 787 11 50 www.aubergelescharmettes.ch
v1 Orsières	4a	Hotel Terminus		+41 (0 27 552 11 00 info@terminus-orsieres.ch www.terminus-orsieres.ch
1/2a	5	Cabane de Mille		+41 (0)27 783 11 82 info@cabanedemille.ch www.cabanedemille.ch
2a/2b	6	Cabane Brunet		+41 (0)27 778 18 10 info@cabanebrunet.ch www.cabanebrunet.ch
2b/3a	7	Cabane FXB Panossière		+41 (0)27 771 33 22 info@panossiere.ch www.panossiere.ch
3a/3b Mauvoisin	8	Hotel de Mauvoisin		+41 (0)27 776 10 22 info@hoteldemauvoisin.com www.hoteldemauvoisin.com
3a/3b (1.7km OR from Mauvoisin)	8a	La Forêt de Mélèzes		info@bonatchiesse.ch www.bonatchiesse.ch
3b/4	9	Cabane de Chanrion		+41 (0)27 778 12 09 info@chanrion.ch www.chanrion.ch
4 Ollomont (3.5km OR)	9a	Dortoir de Ollomont		+39 0165 73220/339 162 9133 info@dortoirdeollomont.it www.dortoirdeollomont.it
4 Ollomont (3.5km OR)	9b	Locanda delle Miniere		+39 0165 189 0722 locandadelleminiere@gmail.com www.locandadelleminiere.it
4 Ollomont (3.5km OR)	9c	La Grandze de François		+39 0165 73339/347 165 5978 info@lagrandzedefrancois. comwww.lagrandzedefrancois.com
4 Ollomont (3.5km OR)	9d	Hotel Mont Gelè		+39 0165 73220 info@montgele.it www.montgele.it
4/5a	10	Rifugio Champillon		+39 320 225 3348 rifugiochampillon@gmail.com www.rifugio-champillon.it

Stage		Name	Facilities	Contact Details
5a/5b St-Rhémy	11	Suisse Locanda di Borgo	Hotel/Private room, WiFi, Drinks, Breakfast, Lunch, Evening Meals	+39 0165 780 901 info@suisselocandadiborgo.it www.suisselocandadiborgo.it
5a/5b St-Rhémy-en-Bosses (2km OR)	12	La Vieille Cloche B&B	Hotel/Private room, WiFi, Breakfast	+39 380 515 9554 info@lavieillecloche.it www.casevacanzavalledaosta.it
5a/5b St-Rhémy-en-Bosses (2km OR)	13	Hotel des Alpes	Hotel/Private room, WiFi, Drinks, Breakfast, Lunch, Evening Meals	+39 0165 780 818 info@desalpeshotel.com www.desalpeshotel.com
5a/5b St-Rhémy-en-Bosses (2km OR)	14	Maison Farinet Chambres d'Hôtes	Hotel/Private room, WiFi, Breakfast	+39 338 1796 046 maisonfarinet@gmail.com www.maisonfarinet.it
5a/5b St-Rhémy-en-Bosses (2km OR)	15	La Thuillettaz B&B	Hotel/Private room, WiFi, Breakfast	+39 335 5243 008 info@thuillettaz.it www.thuillettaz.it
5b/6/v6 Col du Grand-St-Bernard	16	Hotel Italia	Hotel/Private room, WiFi, Drinks, Breakfast, Lunch, Evening Meals	+39 0165 780 063 info@gransanbernardo.it www.gransanbernardo.it
5b/6/v6 Col du Grand-St-Bernard	17	Auberge de l'Hospice	Hotel/Private room, WiFi, Drinks, Breakfast, Lunch, Evening Meals	+41 (0)27 787 11 53 info@aubergehospice.ch www.aubergehospice.ch
5b/6/v6 Col du Grand-St-Bernard	18	l'Hospice du Grand-St-Bernard	Hotel/Private room, Hut/Dormitory, WiFi, Breakfast, Evening Meals	+41 (0)27 787 12 36 hospice@gsbernard.com www.gsbernard.com

Great views of the Mont Blanc Massif (Stage 1/v1/2a)

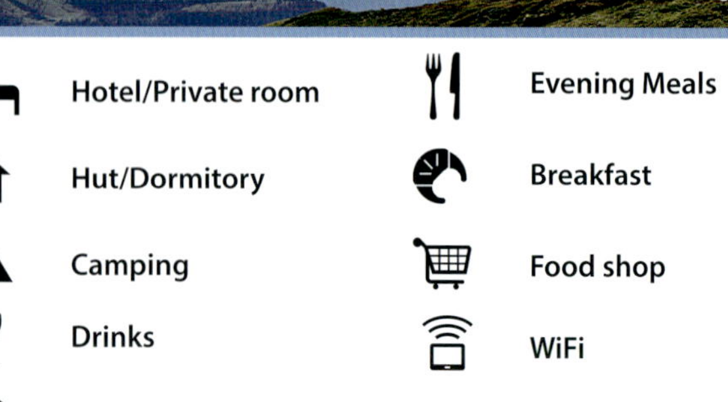

Facilities

Stage	Place	Private Rooms	Dormitory Beds	Campsite	Meals/ Drinks (non-residents)	Grocery Shop	Transport
v1	Orsières	●	●		🍴 🍷	●	🚆 🚌
1/6/v6	Bourg-St-Pierre	●	●	●	🍴 🍷		🚌
1/v1/2a	Cabane de Mille		●		🍴 🍷		
2a/2b	Cabane Brunet		●		🍴 🍷		
2b/3a	Cabane FXB Panossière		●		🍴 🍷		
3a/3b	Mauvoisin	●	●	● (1.7km OR)	🍴 🍷		🚌
3b/4	Cabane de Chanrion		●		🍴 🍷		
4 (3.5km OR)	Ollomont	●	●		🍴 🍷		🚌
4/5a	Rifugio Champillon		●		🍴 🍷		
5a/5b	St-Rhémy	●			🍴 🍷	● (ham/salami only)	
5a/5b (2km OR)	St-Rhémy-en-Bosses	●			🍴 🍷	●	🚌
5b/6/v6	Col du Grand-St-Bernard	●	●		🍴 🍷		🚌

Food

Breakfast: all accommodation (including mountain huts) will provide breakfast. In hotels, there is usually a breakfast buffet which has a wide selection of foods: cereals, bread, fruit, cheese, cold meats, jams and boiled eggs are common. In mountain huts, the choice is more limited and quality varies widely. In some huts, there is little more than a continental breakfast of cereal, bread and jam but in others, this may be supplemented with cold meats and cheese. Coffee and tea are provided: in huts, breakfast coffee may be instant/granulated.

Lunch: there are no grocery shops along the route of the TDC. Furthermore, during the day, you will pass few restaurants and sometimes there are none. Most hikers start the trek with lunch food in their packs to last a few days: when this has been exhausted, they buy packed lunches from huts/hotels. Most accommodation providers can prepare a packed lunch for you: request this the night before. In Swiss and Italian huts, it is not generally acceptable to make up a sandwich for lunch from the breakfast food. You can also buy meals at the hut/hotels if you pass one during the day or, if you arrive early enough at your overnight stop, you can order lunch there: do not miss the plates of cheese and cold meats at Cabane de Chanrion.

Evening meals: most accommodation (including mountain huts) will provide evening meals which are usually hearty three course affairs suitable for weary hikers. A starter, often soup, is normally followed by a main course of meat with vegetables, rice, pasta or salad. This will be rounded off with dessert or cheese. Vegetarian/vegan options will normally be available on request.

Self-catering: there are no grocery shops along the TDC. If you wish to cook for yourself, or you have very specific nutritional requirements, you will need to stock up on supplies before setting out on the trek. However, remember that food is heavy and it may not be wise to start the trek carrying all the food that you will require for the full distance. It is much better to accept at the outset that you can only carry a few days' food than to exhaust yourself in the early stages of the trek by carrying too much. Many campers carry only a small amount of food which they supplement with meals at huts/hotels along the way: make this decision before you start the trek so that you do not carry food that you will not ultimately use.

It is sensible to carry dried food (such as pasta/rice): water is food's heaviest component. Pre-packed freeze-dried meals for backpackers are an excellent choice because they are

The path around Becca de Sery (Stage 2b)

light and are prepared simply by adding boiling water: you can eat them directly out of the bag so there is no washing-up. These days, there are some very tasty meals available from companies like Real Turmat and Firepot. Canned food is not a good choice as it usually has a high water content and is therefore heavy.

How much food do I need?

According to the National Health Service (NHS) in the UK, the recommended daily calorie intake is 2,000 calories for women and 2,500 for men. As you will be expending a lot of energy, it seems sensible to increase this slightly: perhaps a minimum of 2,500 for women and 3,000 for men. Of course, every person has a different metabolism and will have different requirements but this is a good starting point. Also bear in mind that your daily requirement will depend on how far you are planning to hike each day: the further you hike, the more energy you will use and the more food you will need. Remember also to bring a little extra food (over and above your estimated daily requirements) for emergencies.

Suggested daily menu for campers

Breakfast: instant porridge is a good option because it is light and packed with calories. You can get a variety of different flavours. It is also cheap and, in many countries, it is available in supermarkets. You prepare it simply by adding hot water. You can also buy pre-packed freeze-dried breakfast meals: although they are convenient, they are more expensive.

Lunch & snacks during the day: nuts are hard to beat as they are light and packed with energy. Peanuts, for example, have more calories per gram than most other foods. Dried fruit is also good and will help keep your bodily functions regular. Energy bars and candy can help to provide some variety.

Dinner: freeze-dried meals are a good choice. Although they can be expensive, the good quality brands make dinner on the trail something to look forward to. Dried pasta and rice are OK too: you can eat these with packet sauces (prepared by adding water).

Travel to/from the trail-heads

There are five primary trail-heads: in Switzerland, BSP, Mauvoisin and Col du GSB are along the route of the trek and Orsières is a short distance OR; in Italy, the village of St-Rhémy is on the route. The four Swiss trail-heads are served directly by public transport, however, the Italian trail-head is not.

Primary trail-head	Public transport to trail-head
Orsières	**From/to Switzerland:** Orsières is connected to the Swiss rail network. It is at the S end of a branch line which travels to/from Martigny. You can also travel by train between Orsières and le Châble (which has buses to Mauvoisin). See **www.sbb.ch** or **www.postauto.ch.** **From/to Italy:** TMR bus 12.211 travels between Orsières and Aosta through the GSB Tunnel. Mon-Fri; **www.tmrsa.ch.**
Bourg-St-Pierre	**From/to Switzerland:** take the train to Orsières. Then bus B210 connects Orsières and BSP (25min): buses normally connect with the train. See **www.sbb.ch** or **www.postauto.ch.** **From/to Italy:** TMR bus 12.211 travels between BSP and Aosta through the GSB Tunnel; Mon-Fri.
Mauvoisin	**From/to Switzerland:** take the train to le Châble. Then bus B253 runs from le Châble to Mauvoisin (45min): buses normally connect with the train. Daily.
Col du GSB	**From/to Switzerland:** take the train to Orsières. Then bus B210 travels between Orsières and Col du GSB (via BSP; 50min): buses normally connect with the train. Daily.
St-Rhémy	No public transport directly to St-Rhémy. However, Arriva (**www.arriva.it/en**) runs a bus (Mon-Sat) between Aosta and St-Rhémy-en-Bosses: from there, it is 45min (2km) on foot to St-Rhémy. For travel to/from Aosta, see below.

Travel to Switzerland

Because the TDC is easier to access by public transport from the Swiss side, it is best to fly to Switzerland. Geneva Airport has flights to/from many cities in Europe, North America and other parts of the world. Geneva Airport has a train station: from there, it takes around 3-3.5hr to travel to the Swiss trail-heads by train/bus (see p26). Zurich Airport also operates international flights: trains from Zurich Airport to the trail-heads take 4.5-5.5hr.

You can buy Swiss train and bus tickets together (in a single transaction) at the airports or online at **www.sbb.ch** or using SBB's efficient smart-phone app. For timetables and route maps, see **www.sbb.ch**, **www.postauto.ch** or **www.tmrsa.ch.**

Travel to Italy

Travelling to the trail-heads from the Italian side is more difficult. The nearest international airport to the TDC is Turin. Trains travel from Turin to Aosta (22km from St-Rhémy), however, because there is no train station at the airport, you first have to travel by bus/taxi from Turin Airport to one of the two main stations in Turin city centre: Turin Porta Susa or Turin Porta Nuova. After reaching Aosta, you will then need to take a bus to St-Rhémy-en-Bosses (45min; **www.arriva.it/en**): from there, it is 2km on foot to the trail-head at St-Rhémy. Alternatively, take a taxi directly from Aosta to St-Rhémy (30min). You could also fly to Milan Malpensa, Milan Linate or Milan Bergamo. To get to St-Rhémy from Milan or Bergamo, first take the train to Turin: from there, follow the instructions above. For train timetables and tickets, see **www.trenitalia.com**.

Travel between Switzerland and Italy

TMR operates bus 12.211 (Mon-Fri) between Martigny (Switzerland) and Aosta (Italy). It travels via Sembrancher, Orsières and BSP. However, because it uses the GSB Tunnel, it does not cross Col du GSB. Because this service takes only 1hr to travel between Aosta and the Swiss trail-head at BSP, those arriving at the TDC from the Italian side may find it more straightforward to start the trek at BSP rather than St-Rhémy (which is harder to access). Alternatively, those finishing the TDC at BSP could use this bus service to travel into Italy after the trek. For timetables, see **www.tmrsa.ch**.

Travel by car & trail-head parking

Because the TDC is circular, you could park a car at various points along the route and then return to it at the end of the trek. Around the village of BSP, there is plenty of parking: alternatively, you could park near ① along Stage 6. There is a small parking area at Mauvoisin too. Col du GSB is a busy place straddling two different countries and it can be difficult to establish which parking rule applies to which parking spaces: some of the parking is short term only but for other spaces, the position is not always clear. However, below the col, on the Italian side, between ① and ②, there is a large parking area where you can leave your car for many days (free of charge). St-Rhémy only has a couple of parking spaces and it does not seem fair on local residents to hog them for a long period: however, 1.5km N of St-Rhémy, you will find a large parking area right beside the route of the TDC.

Cabane FXB Panossière (Stage 2b/3a)

On the Trail

Mont Vélan & Grand Combin (Stage 4)

Costs & budgeting

No permits are required to hike the TDC. However, trekking in Switzerland is slightly more expensive than in other parts of the Alps: food and public transport in particular are fairly costly, however, what you get for your money is normally good quality. In Italy, both food and public transport are cheaper than in Switzerland.

Prices in mountain huts have risen greatly over the last decade but we think that they still offer good value when you consider the high cost of getting supplies to the remote locations. The cost of half-board (breakfast, dinner and a dormitory bed) in huts varies widely: in Swiss huts, you will pay CHF68-95; in Rifugio Champillon in Italy, it is around €70. Only Cabane de Chanrion offers a discount to alpine club members. In hotels along the TDC, double/twin rooms (for 2 people including breakfast) cost around CHF150/€120 in total. By camping and/or cooking for yourself, you could save a lot of money.

	Approximate Cost (subject to change) Switzerland/Italy
Half-board in mountain hut (dormitory bed, breakfast & dinner)	**CHF68-95/€70**
Double room in hotel	From **CHF150/€120** upwards (for 2 people sharing a double/twin room)
Half-board at l'Hospice du GSB (dormitory bed, breakfast & dinner)	**€65**
Campsite	**CHF16-22/€10-20** per person
Main course in restaurant	**CHF20-40/€12-25**
Beer (0.5L)	**CHF6-8/€6-8**

Weather

The Alps have a relatively dry and predictable climate compared to mountains in the UK for example: clear and sunny skies are common during the hiking season. However, conditions can still change quickly so be prepared for high winds, rain, low cloud and poor visibility. Furthermore, snow is always possible on cols and summits, even in summer. Sometimes you might experience a mixture of conditions during the day: perhaps some sun and clear skies for a time with cloud and/or rain during other parts of the day. Always remember that mountains can be dangerous so treat them with respect and caution, even if the weather forecast is favourable.

The region has several micro-climates with the weather often differing from valley to valley. It is possible therefore to find blazing sunshine on one side of a ridge and cloud/rain over the other side.

If you can, obtain a weather forecast on your smartphone before setting out each day. MeteoSwiss, the Swiss meteorological office, provides national, regional and local forecasts at **www.meteoswiss.admin.ch**. It also has an excellent smartphone app which provides regularly updated local forecasts. For the Italian parts of the TDC, the smartphone app Meteo.it is useful. Many other internet sites and apps also provide forecasts, with a varying degree of reliability. If you are unable to obtain a forecast on your smartphone then it is sensible to speak to the hut wardens: their understanding of local weather conditions can be invaluable and you should follow their advice if they tell you it is not safe to hike. Local forecasts are also displayed at tourist information offices and huts.

Paths and waymarking

Paths and tracks on the TDC are generally well-maintained and straightforward to walk upon but there are rocky, challenging sections too. The terrain undulates regularly and some sections are steep and/or exposed: sometimes drops are sheer and occasionally, ropes/chains have been fixed to the rocks for safety. Some paths can be muddy and slippery after rain.

Generally, the route is well marked and navigation is usually straightforward in good conditions: there are often waymarks and signs to assist. However, occasionally paths are less easy to follow and navigation is more difficult: for example, where the trail crosses rocky zones. In Switzerland, waymarks are red/white stripes or yellow/black diamonds. In Italy, there are yellow/black diamonds and yellow arrows. Waymarks tend to be placed sparingly to avoid sullying the natural environment with man-made marks: often they are found only where absolutely necessary to prevent deviation from the route. A red/white cross on a rock or a tree indicates that you are off the TDC route. Yellow signposts often display times and/or distances to specific destinations: the timings are not always reliable.

Swiss waymark
Swiss waymark
Italian waymark
Typical yellow sign

In the route descriptions, we do not highlight every junction because the waymarking is usually good: generally, we only mention junctions if they are particularly significant or if there are no waymarks. As a rule of thumb, remain on the main path unless instructed otherwise by signs/waymarks on the ground or the maps/route descriptions in this book: however, keep your wits about you because there will of course be the occasional exception to this rule! Also, bear in mind that waymarking is at the mercy of the environment: for example, signs and waymarks are sometimes blown down or destroyed by snow.

On the high points of the TDC, snow can remain into July, covering paths and making progress/route-finding more difficult: follow waymarks carefully because they can be hard to spot against the snow. Normally, early in the season, the trail will become quickly tracked by others ahead of you but always be wary of following someone else's footprints: there is a good chance that they are on the correct path but it is obviously possible that they may have strayed from the trail. Also, remember that any fresh snow will obscure footprints.

If you see mountain biking signs, sometimes indicated by the letters 'VTT' (Vélo Tout Terrain), then take care: mountain bikes are fast and often quiet and a collision between a walker and a mountain bike could be serious.

Maps

In this book, we have included maps for the entire TDC: each stage has 1:40,000 scale maps produced by Knife Edge Outdoor Guidebooks. Because we were unable to find commercially available maps that suited our purposes, we commissioned our own topographical maps: they are perfect for both planning and navigation while on the trek.

However, we also recommend obtaining our sheet map for the TDC: '***Trekking Map: Tour des Combins***' (ISBN 9781912933525). It has a 1:40,000 scale, covers the entire trek, clearly shows the route and can be used seamlessly with this book. A sheet map makes it easier to plan the trek, navigate in poor conditions and identify peaks along the trail. Our map is available from **www.knifeedgeoutdoor.com**, online retailers and many shops. It is best to buy this map before leaving home, because there are so few shops in the region. The only other sheet maps with a larger scale are the 1:25,000 maps made by Swisstopo: however, you will need four of these maps to cover the entire TDC: 1345 Orsières, 1346 Chanrion, 1366 Mont Vélan and 1365 Grand-St-Bernard. Swisstopo also produces a 1:50,000 map that covers the entire route (5003 Mont Blanc-Grand Combin), however, the scale is smaller than our map and it can be hard to find in shops. Unlike the Knife Edge map, the Swisstopo maps do not specifically highlight the TDC route.

Storing bags

If you wish to spend some time elsewhere after the trek, then you will probably have additional baggage which you need to store while trekking. The TDC is a circular route and therefore you will return to your starting point at the end of the trek. Normally, a hotel that you have stayed at before starting the trek will store your bags until your return: some may charge extra for this so check when booking.

At Geneva Airport and Geneva Cornavin stations, there are manned baggage counters (near the SBB Travel Centres) where you can leave luggage for CHF12/day. However, you can only deposit/reclaim baggage during the travel centre's opening hours. Zurich Airport also has manned luggage storage.

There are also unmanned luggage lockers at many large Swiss train stations (including Geneva Airport station, Geneva Cornavin and Zurich). However, the maximum storage time is 96 hours which will be insufficient for most trekkers.

Baggage transfer

Due to the remoteness of the huts along the TDC, baggage transfer services are not available on the TDC.

Fuel for camping stoves

Airlines will not permit the transport of fuel so campers will need to source it upon arrival, before setting out on the trek. Standard screw-in gas canisters and Campingaz canisters (pierceable and twist-on) are usually available in Switzerland and Italy: outdoor shops normally stock them and you may find them in supermarkets, grocery shops and campsites in the region. However, there is nowhere to buy gas along the TDC so source it before arriving at the trail-head. If you need petrol/diesel for a multi-fuel stove, there are service stations at Orsières and BSP.

Outdoor shops

The nearest outdoor shop to the TDC is **Cristal Sport** in Orsières: +41 (0)27 783 2440; info@cristalsport.ch; www.cristalsport.ch. It is useful if, like many, you arrive in Orsières by train. Further away, there are a few outdoor shops in Martigny:

- **Look Montagne:** Rue du Léman 19, 1920 Martigny; +41 (0)27 722 9155; www.lookmontagne.ch

- **Sport X:** Av. de Fully 63, 1920 Martigny; +41 (0)27 720 6882; www.sportx.ch

However, those arriving at Geneva Airport may find it more convenient to visit one of the outdoor shops in Geneva city centre: trains from Geneva Airport to Orsières stop at Geneva Cornavin which is close to the following stores:

- **Decathlon:** Rue de Lausanne 16-20, 1201 Geneva; +41 (0)22 900 0404; www.decathlon.ch
- **Univers Sports:** Rue de la Servette 52, 1202 Genève; +41 (0)22 733 3358; www.univers-sports.ch
- **Ochsner Sport:** Rue du Marché 9/11, 1204 Geneva; +41 (0)22 310 8968; www.ochsnersport.ch

On the Italian side of the TDC, the closest outdoor shops are located in Aosta:

- **Mountain Shop Aosta:** Via Jean Baptiste de Tillier 21, 11100 Aosta AO; +39 0165 361 465; www.mountain-shop.com
- **Meinardi Sport:** Via Edouard Aubert 27, 11100 Aosta AO; +39 0165 40 678
- **CMP:** Via Edouard Aubert 49, 11100 Aosta AO; +39 0165 231 693; www.cmpsport.com

Drinking water

Drinking water should be one of your primary considerations each day. The sun in the Alps is extremely strong: dehydration and sunstroke are possibilities and you will need more water than usual (perhaps three to four litres per day). Tap water is drinkable and you should fill up your bottles each morning before you depart: it is good practice to start the day with at least two litres. Along the trail, you can fill up at the fountains, bars and shops in villages/towns or from the many streams and rivers: plan carefully so that you know where the next water point is and always check your water levels when you pass a water point.

Remember that the volume of water in streams may vary depending upon the season and the amount of rainfall over previous weeks and months: at the start of the season (June), the rivers are usually in full flow but by the end of the season (September), many of the smaller ones may be dry. Although some do it, we do not recommend drinking water from a river, stream or lake, without first dealing with possible contaminants including visible particulates, bacteria, viruses, protozoa (for example, giardia) and parasites.

It is possible to deal with most contaminants using one or more of the methods described below but you should research thoroughly the specific product you are planning to use to understand its effectiveness and any possible risks:

- **Boiling** is the traditional method. A rolling boil of 1min should kill everything in the water. However, it does not remove visible particulates so the boiled water will remain the same colour as when you found it, which can be off-putting. It also uses up a lot of fuel and takes time so is impractical.
- **Filtering** usually removes visible particulates, working miracles by turning coloured water clear. It also normally removes around 99.9% of bacteria, protozoa and parasites. Filters are often cheap and light. It is the quickest method of treatment so it is useful for long-distance routes. However, most filters cannot remove viruses (although these are unlikely to be an issue on this trek): if you are concerned about viruses then you will need to invest in one of the more expensive filters that remove them or combine filtering with another method (boiling, UV or chemical treatment).

- **Chemical treatment** can remove bacteria, protozoa, viruses and parasites: each product is different so read the labels carefully. However, there are many disadvantages to chemicals: they do not remove visible particulates so the water will remain the same colour as when you found it; water treated with chemicals often has a taste (although you can usually buy different chemicals to deal with that); the water usually cannot be drunk immediately as chemicals take time to kill pathogens; and from a health perspective, consuming chemicals may not be good for you.
- **UV treatment** kills bacteria, protozoa, viruses and parasites. However, it does not remove visible particulates so the water will remain the same colour as when you found it: coloured water can be off-putting and the UV treatment is less effective if the water is not completely clear. That said, coloured water is not usually a problem on this trek. The most common products are Steripens which are very light.

Perhaps the most practical single method for this trek is filtering: because virus contamination is unlikely, many hikers drink water which has only been filtered with a standard filter, running a small risk of virus contamination. However, if you prefer to be more cautious, you could combine filtration with UV treatment (using a Steripen): this removes or kills practically everything.

The actual effectiveness of individual products varies and is beyond the scope of this book so do your research beforehand. However, it is worth noting that many products claim to be 99.9% effective indicating that drinking water from wild sources can never be said to be 100% risk free. You will have to weigh up the risks and make up your own mind. You drink the water at your own risk!

	Visible Particulates	Bacteria	Virus	Protozoa	Parasites
Boiling	✗	✓	✓	✓	✓
Filter	✓	✓	Only top of the range filters remove viruses	✓	✓
Chemical Treatment	✗	✓	✓	✓	✓
UV Treatment (such as Steripen)	✗	✓	✓	✓	✓

If, like many, you do decide to drink from natural sources then, as well as treating the water, there are a few rules that you should follow to reduce further any risk:

- Avoid water where there is evidence nearby of animals, especially cows or sheep: carcasses (of dead animals) or faeces can cause contamination
- Do not collect water downstream from buildings or grazing areas
- Preferably drink from moving water. The faster the better
- The bigger the river/stream the better
- Generally the higher the altitude the better

Ticks

As is often the case in Europe, ticks are present in the Alps. They can carry Lyme disease or tick-borne encephalitis so check yourself regularly. Remove ticks with a tick removal tool (making sure that you get all of it out) and then disinfect the area.

Escape Routes

The TDC has a few points with road access, enabling you to leave the route early: BSP, Mauvoisin, St-Rhémy and Col du GSB. However, the availability of public transport at these locations varies (see p26). Furthermore, on many other parts of the trek, you could descend into the valleys if you needed to: there are usually roads there. However, on the remote parts of Stages 3b and 4, escape would be more difficult.

Pastous

A Pastou keeping watch over its flock

The trail enters rural areas and sheep are grazed in the high mountains in summer. Often, the shepherd will live at high altitude in a tiny cabin throughout the grazing season. To protect the sheep from wolves (which are now prevalent again), flocks are often accompanied by dogs. Frequently, the dog is a Pastou (or Patou) which is very large, white and long-haired: it is related to an old Pyrenean breed. They are usually raised with the flock so form a close bond with the sheep. Often they growl or bark if you approach the flock. Although uncommon, occasionally visitors to the Alps are bitten by a Pastou which thought that there was a threat to its sheep. Accordingly, the best advice is to give them a wide berth and assume that there may be a Pastou with any flock. Remember that from afar, the colour and texture of Pastous' coats makes them hard to spot amongst the sheep.

Approaching Col du Bastillon (Stage v6)

Equipment

Passarelle de Corbassière (Stage 2b)

The trekker has no influence over challenges like weather and terrain but can control the contents of a pack carried on the trail. Because there are no baggage transfer services on the TDC, you will have to carry all your own gear and many trekkers set off carrying equipment which is unnecessary or simply too heavy. The more your pack weighs, the harder the trek will be: lugging a heavy pack can lead to exhaustion, injury and/or abandonment. Accordingly, you should give equipment choice careful consideration: it will be crucial to your enjoyment of the trek and the likelihood of success.

Of course, it is easy to understand why a pack should be light, however, it is much more difficult to put this into practice when there are so many things you 'need' in daily life. With experience, it becomes easier to sift between essentials and luxuries but, if you have not been on a multi-day trek before, this can be an unfathomable dilemma. However, if you follow the advice here and limit yourself to the items on our checklist then you should not go far wrong.

A trekker's base weight is the weight of his/her pack, excluding food and water. If you are not carrying camping gear and cooking equipment, it is perfectly possible to get by with a base weight of 5-6kg (13lb) or less. If you intend to carry camping equipment then, by investing in some modern lightweight gear, you could start the trek with a base weight of 8-9kg (17lb) or less. Many people are quick to tell you that the lighter the gear, the greater the price but that is not always the case. While it is true that lightweight gear can be expensive, there are also some excellent lightweight products which are great value. Tents, sleeping bags and backpacks are the three heaviest items that you will carry so they offer the biggest opportunities for weight-saving. But do not ignore the smaller items either as the weight can quickly add up. Accordingly, if you can afford it, it is sensible to invest some money in gear before you leave home. The lighter your gear, the more you will enjoy the trek and the better your chance of success. Be ruthless as every ounce counts.

Recommended basic kit

When undertaking any long-distance route, you should be properly equipped for the worst terrain and the worst weather conditions which you could encounter. In the Alps, this means that you should carry clothing to combat cold, heat, sun, and rain. Becoming cold and wet in the mountains is unpleasant and can be dangerous. Furthermore, if you are lucky and the sun does shine, you will not want to get sunburn (which can put an end to your trek). Also remember that, even in summer, you could experience snow at altitude.

Layering of clothing is the key to managing body temperature. In cool weather, layers can be added: warm air becomes trapped between the layers, acting as insulation. In warmer weather, you simply remove layers and carry them in your pack. Merino wool or man-made materials are preferable: they are lightweight and warm and they wick moisture away from the skin. Do not wear cotton: it is heavy and it does not dry quickly (making you cold). Always carry a spare set of clothes in case you get wet.

Boots/Shoes	Good quality, properly fitting and worn in. Robust soles (such as Vibram) are advisable. Some use trail-running shoes but many prefer boots with ankle support. Shoes/boots with a waterproof membrane (such as Gore-Tex) are good, particularly if there is snow on the ground.	
Socks	2 pairs of good quality, quick-drying walking socks.	
Camp shoes	It is nice to have spare footwear for the evenings. Flip-flops or Crocs are a common choice as they are light. However, if you have comfortable hiking boots/shoes then you might consider not bringing camp shoes to save weight.	
Waterproof jacket and trousers	They should be waterproof and breathable.	
Base layers	2 T-shirts and underpants of man-made fabrics or merino wool, which wick moisture away from your body.	
Fleece	A warm middle layer. Man-made fabrics are best.	
Trousers/shorts	1 pair of lightweight walking trousers and 1 pair of shorts. Alternatively, some prefer 2 pairs of trousers. Convertible trousers are practical as you can remove the legs on warm days.	
Gloves	Lightweight gloves are usually sufficient. However, it is sensible to choose waterproof ones.	
Warm hat & buff	Even in summer it can be cold at altitude, particularly on windy days.	
Down jacket	Even in summer, prepare for low temperatures, especially in the evening and early morning.	
Sunglasses, sun hat, sunscreen and lip salve	The sun in the Alps is strong: do not set out without these items.	
Sleeping sheet	A thin bag made of silk or cotton. Required to sleep in mountain huts.	
Head-light with spare batteries	A flashlight is useful (in both huts and tents) if you need to go to the bathroom in the night. Furthermore, it is good practice to carry one for emergencies: it can assist if you get caught out late and enable you to signal to rescuers.	

Backpack	Your backpack is one of the heaviest items that you will carry. The difference in the weights of various packs can be surprisingly large. 35-40 litres should be sufficient if you are not carrying camping gear. 45-60 litres should be adequate for campers. If you need a pack bigger than these then you are most likely carrying too much. Look for well-padded shoulder straps and waist band. Much of the weight of the pack should sit on your hips rather than your shoulders.
Waterproof pack-liner	Most backpacks are not very waterproof. An internal liner will keep your gear dry if it rains. Many trekkers use external pack covers but we do not find them to be very useful: they flap in the wind and, in heavy rain, water still leaks into the pack around the straps (so you need an internal liner anyway).
Basic first-aid kit	Including plasters, a bandage, antiseptic wipes and painkillers. Blister plasters, moleskin padding or tape (such as Leukotape) can be useful to prevent or combat blisters. A tick removal tool or card is also recommended.
Map, compass & GPS device	For maps, see p30. A GPS unit or a smart-phone mapping app is a useful addition but they are no substitute for a map and compass: after all, batteries can run out and electronics can fail.
Walking poles	These transfer weight from your legs onto your arms, keeping you fresher. They also save your knees (particularly on descents) and can reduce the likelihood of falling or twisting an ankle. Poles are invaluable in snowy conditions.
Phone and charging cable	A smartphone is a very useful tool on a trek. It can be used for emergencies. Furthermore, apps for weather, mapping and hotel booking are invaluable. It can also serve as your camera, saving weight.
Ziplock plastic bag	A lightweight way of keeping money and passports dry.
Ear plugs	Useful if staying in huts: you will thank us if someone snores!
Emergency food	Carry some emergency food over and above your planned daily rations. Energy bars, nuts and dried fruit are all good.
Toilet paper and trowel	Bring a backpacking trowel in case nature calls on the trail: bury toilet waste and carry out used toilet paper.
Whistle	For emergencies. Many rucksacks have one incorporated into the sternum strap.
Knife	Such as a Swiss Army knife.
Portable battery pack	Although huts have charging points for electronic devices, they will be in high demand. Accordingly, many people carry their own battery packs: Anker make good ones.
Toiletries	If you wish to take showers at campsites and huts, a small hotel-size bottle of shower gel should be enough to last the trek, saving weight. An almost empty toothpaste tube will also save weight. Leave that make-up behind!
Towel	A lightweight trekking towel is a good idea if you wish to take showers at campsites or huts.

Additional gear for campers

Tent: this is one of the heaviest things that you will carry so it provides a big opportunity for weight saving. Some 2-person tents weigh more than 3kg while others weigh less than 0.6kg. The heaviest ones are normally built for extreme winter conditions and are overkill for the normal Alpine trekking season. Some of the lightest ones, however, are not particularly robust and the thin material can be prone to damage on rocky ground.

Although a few premium brands charge a lot for their products and there are some very expensive tents at the lightest end of the scale, these days there are plenty of mid-weight tents available at reasonable prices. Tents weighing 1 to 1.6kg often strike a good balance between price, longevity and weight. Consider money spent here as an investment in your well-being and enjoyment of one of the world's great trails. Believe us when we say that a few kgs can be the difference between success and failure.

Your tent should be waterproof to ensure that you stay dry during rainy nights. A footprint is a good idea to protect its base: 'footprint' is a trendy, modern word for what used to be known as a groundsheet. Sometimes you can buy footprints specific to your tent model but we prefer to use a sheet of Tyvek which can be cut to size: Tyvek is extremely tough and is cheaper, and normally lighter, than most branded footprints.

Tent pegs: tent weights provided by manufacturers normally exclude the weight of the pegs. The pegs actually provided with tents tend to be quite heavy and many trekkers buy replacement ones which are lighter. Six heavy pegs can weigh as much as 240g while 6 light pegs can weigh as little as 6g. There are many different types available these days and it is important to match the peg with the type of ground they will be used in. You will usually find grassy pitches on this trek, and therefore pegs do not need to be overly strong: titanium ones (which are very light) are a good choice although they can be expensive.

Sleeping bag: every sleeping bag has a 'comfort rating': this is the lowest temperature at which the standard woman should enjoy a comfortable night's sleep. There is also a 'lower comfort limit' which is for men. That may sound simple but it is not. Although all reputable sleeping bag manufacturers use the same independent standard, the bags are not tested in the same place so there is a lack of consistency amongst ratings. Also, the ratings are designed with an average man and woman in mind, however, every person is different: some people get colder than others and need a warmer bag. The ratings should therefore be used as a guide only and it is wise to choose a bag with a comfort rating which is at least 5°C lower than the night temperatures that you are likely to encounter.

Between the start of July and the middle of August, a bag with a comfort rating between -5°C and 5°C (depending on whether you sleep hot or cold) is normally sufficient to cope with the likely night temperatures. Outside of this period, it can be prudent to go with something a little warmer in case the weather throws a cold spell at you: perhaps a bag with a comfort rating between -10°C and 0°C. It is quite a difficult decision because although you want to be warm at night, you do not want to bring a bag that is much too warm as that would add unnecessary weight to your pack.

Unfortunately, with sleeping bags, price tends to be inversely proportional to weight. This is largely because the lightest bags are filled with goose/duck down which is expensive. Synthetic bags are also available but they are much heavier so down is a better choice for trekking. The disadvantage of down bags is that they can lose their warmth if they get wet but that is less likely if you have a good tent and pack liner. Our advice is first to decide what comfort rating you will require. Then choose the lightest bag (with that rating) which you can afford.

Sleeping mat: this makes it comfortable for you to sleep on the hard ground and insulates you from the ground's cold surface. There are three types: air, self-inflating and closed-cell foam. The advantages and disadvantages of each are set out below. All factors considered, we prefer air mats although the very lightest ones may not be sufficiently warm for some trekkers. Thermarest's NeoAir Xlite and NeoAir Xtherm are good choices.

Sleeping mat type	Pros	Cons
Air mats: need to be blown up	Lightest **Very comfortable** Most compact when packed **Thicker: good for side sleepers**	Most expensive **Hard work to inflate** Can be punctured **Less warm than self-inflating**
Self-inflating mats: a combination of air and closed-cell foam. The mat partially inflates itself when the valve is opened	Warmest **Very comfortable** Quite compact **More durable than air mats** Firmness is adjustable by adding air	Heavier **More expensive than closed-cell foam** Can be punctured
Closed-cell foam mats	Light **Least expensive** Most durable **Cannot be punctured**	Not compact: needs to be strapped to the outside of your pack **Least warm** Least comfortable

Pillow: some use rolled-up clothing but we prefer inflatable trekking pillows which only weigh around 50g.

Stove: you should choose a stove that uses a type of fuel which is readily available in the Alps. Airlines do not permit you to carry fuel on planes so, if you are flying, you will need to source fuel on arrival. Although white gas/Coleman fuel is sometimes stocked in outdoor shops, these days gas is more widely available (see p30). Most gas stoves are designed to fit generic screw-on canisters which are readily available in Europe. Canisters for Campinggaz stoves (which are popular in France) are widely available too. Multi-fuel stoves that burn petrol and/or diesel are useful but they tend to be heavier, dirtier and more complicated than many gas stoves: the locations of service stations are listed on p30.

Hundreds of different stoves are available, some more complicated than others. Often the lightest ones are the most simple and often the most simple ones are relatively inexpensive. If, like most campers, you will eat dried food such as pasta and rice then your stove will need to do little more than boil water. A basic stove which mounts on top of a gas canister will therefore be adequate: such a stove should also be cheap and lightweight (less than 100g).

Pots: if, like most campers, you will eat dried food such as pasta and rice then you will only need one pot which will do little more than boil water. To save weight, go for the smallest pot that you can get away with. For example, if you are travelling solo and planning to use freeze-dried backpacking meals then you would need nothing bigger than a 500-600ml pot. Titanium pots are usually the lightest but they are slightly more expensive. Get the lightest one that you can afford.

Fork/Spoon: we love Sporks! They have a spoon at one end and a fork at the other. They weigh only 9g and cost very little.

Descending towards Val d'Entremont (Stage v6)

Safety

The road to Col du GSB (Stage 5b)

On a calm summer's day the Alps are paradise. But a sudden weather shift or an injury can alter your circumstances dramatically so treat the mountains with respect and be conscious of your experience levels and physical capabilities. The following is a non-exhaustive list of recommendations:

- The fitter you are at the start of your trip, the more you will enjoy the hiking.
- Start early to avoid ascending during the hottest part of the day and to allow more surplus time in case something goes wrong.
- Do not stray from the waymarked paths so as to avoid getting lost and to help prevent erosion of the landscape.
- Before you set out each day, study the route and make plans based upon the abilities of the weakest member of your party.
- Obtain a weather forecast (daily if possible) and reassess your plans in light of it. Avoid exposed routes if the weather is uncertain.
- Never be too proud to turn back if you find the going too tough or if the weather deteriorates.
- Bring a map and compass and know how to use them. GPS devices are useful too.
- It can be sensible to call ahead to your accommodation and tell them what time you will arrive. If you do not turn up then they can raise the alarm.
- Carry surplus food and clothing for emergencies.
- Avoid exposed high ground in a thunderstorm. If you get caught out in one then drop your walking poles and stay away from trees, overhanging rocks, metal structures and caves. Generally accepted advice is to squat on your pack and keep as low as possible.
- In snowy conditions, follow waymarks carefully and do not leave the route. Be wary of following someone else's footprints: there is always a chance that they have strayed from the trail.
- In the event of an accident, move an injured person into a safe place and administer any necessary first-aid. Keep the victim warm. If possible, use your cell-phone to call for help: for emergency numbers, see p41. If you have no signal then send someone to the nearest mountain hut or settlement for help.
- Mountain biking is now very popular in the Alps so watch out. A collision with a bike would not be pleasant.
- When cooking on a camping stove, place the stove on the ground. Avoid using it on a picnic table. We have witnessed a trekker knocking over his stove and spilling boiling water on his legs: this is a sure-fire way to end your trek.

General Information

Language: in the parts of Switzerland which the TDC travels, French is the first language but many locals will have, at least, some basic English. German and Italian are also official languages in Switzerland and are widely spoken in the Valais. In Italy's Aosta Valley, Italian is the first language but many locals also speak French and/or some English.

Charging electronic devices: almost all accommodation provides charging facilities: in mountain huts, you may have to queue and therefore some trekkers also bring their own portable battery packs. In Italy, continental two pin plugs are used. In Switzerland, these days, most tourist accommodation also provides continental two pin sockets: older properties may still have the traditional three pin sockets but these are becoming more rare. Travellers from outside the EU should get by in both countries with a Type-C Europlug adapter.

Money: Italy uses the Euro (€). Switzerland has the Swiss Franc (CHF) but Euros are normally accepted too (although you may not get a great exchange rate). There are no ATMs along the route of the TDC: the closest ATM is at Orsières. However, it is sensible to withdraw cash before reaching Orsières in case the ATM is out of order. Hotels and most huts accept credit cards, however, Rifugio Champillon only accepts cash. It is a good idea to carry additional cash in case credit card machines in remote locations are out of order.

Visas: citizens of the UK, EU, Australia, New Zealand, Canada or the US do not need a visa for short tourist trips to Switzerland or Italy.

Cell-phones: these days, there is cell network along most of the trail (particularly in towns and villages). However, in some remote valleys, network coverage is poor. When network is available, it is likely to be a 4G/5G service, enabling access to the internet from smart-phones.

International dialling codes: the country codes for Italy and Switzerland are +39 and +41 respectively. If dialling from overseas, the first 0 in Swiss area codes is omitted. However, the 0 in Italian area codes is not omitted.

WiFi: most hotels have WiFi. Some huts have WiFi but some do not.

Emergencies and rescue: the emergency number is 144 in Switzerland and 118 in Italy. However, you can also use 112 which is the universal European emergency number. Rescue services in Switzerland and Italy's Aosta Valley are not always free of charge. In particular, helicopter evacuation could cost you a lot of money. Accordingly, it is wise to take out your own rescue insurance. A good option is the British section of the Austrian Alpine Club (which is open to everyone and not just British trekkers): see **www.alpenverein.at/britannia**. Membership costs £62 and includes worldwide rescue insurance: it also gives you a CHF15 discount on the price of a bed at Cabane de Chanrion.

Medical insurance: depending upon your nationality, any required medical treatment in Switzerland/Italy may not be provided free of charge so it is wise to purchase travel/medical insurance which covers hiking: this is not the same as rescue insurance.

Tourist information: the following websites are useful:

- **www.myswitzerland.com:** the official tourism website for **Switzerland**
- **www.lovevda.it:** the official tourism website for the **Aosta Valley**
- **www.sbb.ch:** the official website **Swiss Rail**. You can search bus/train timetables and buy tickets
- **www.sac-cas.ch:** the official website for the **Swiss Alpine Club**

Wildlife

Ibex on the TDC (Stage 3a)

The extremely varied ecosystems mean that there are plenty of vertebrates in the Alps. Generally, early morning is the best time for sightings: often the first party on the trail may see many chamois or ibex but following groups will not see any.

Bouquetin (ibex): a member of the goat family with long scimitar shaped horns (which have deep ridges). It was saved from extinction by the Savoy kings who banned most hunting in 1821 and created a royal reserve in 1856 (which finally became Italy's Gran Paradiso National Park). After a series of reintroductions in the 20th century, they are now fairly widespread throughout the Alps.

Chamois: another type of mountain goat which is smaller than the ibex and is widespread in the Alps. It has shorter horns which do not have deep ridges. Chamois are frequently spotted in herds. They are much more wary of humans than ibex.

Deer: various species are common below the tree line. Chevreuil (roe deer) are reddish or grey-brown and daim (fallow deer) tend to be brown with white spots. Look out for them when climbing through forests early in the morning.

Marmots: everyone loves these fat rodents which are easily spotted in summer when they graze relentlessly to put on layers of fat to last the long winter hibernation. They live in colonies in grassy parts of the mountains, often standing upright on their hind legs like a meerkat. They whistle as you approach to warn their colony of an intruder.

Marmot

Sanglier (wild boar): a member of the pig family with small tusks. They are common in forests. In the unlikely event that you spot one, keep your distance because they can be dangerous.

Wolves: they were hunted almost to extinction in the Alps in the 20th century. In recent decades, conservation efforts in Italy increased numbers and many have crossed the border into neighbouring countries through the mountains. They are protected but their presence is controversial and particularly unpopular with shepherds who lose sheep to them. They are rarely spotted by hikers.

Other mammals: squirrels, foxes, badgers, weasels and mice are fairly common below the tree line.

Fish: species of trout are found in many rivers, streams and lakes. Some high alpine lakes also contain Arctic char.

Lagopède (or ptarmigan): a grouse-like bird. Its plumage is white in the winter and largely brown in the summer.

Golden eagle

Golden eagle: during the hot parts of the day they can sometimes be seen circling in the thermals to gain altitude as they scan the ground for prey.

Gypaète barbu (bearded vulture): a vulture with a wingspan of up to 3m. In Germany it was given the name 'Lammergeier' (lamb-hawk) because it was believed that it attacked lambs. It is the largest bird in the Alps. Although rare, numbers have increased in recent years.

Sheep grazing along the TDC (Stage 5b)

Plants and Flowers

A flower-filled alpine meadow in June

The Alps are home to thousands of species of plants including the incredible wild-flowers. June is a fabulous month for flowers, which wait patiently throughout the winter for the snow to clear and then rapidly spring to life. At this time, carpets of different colours cover the slopes and pastures. Although spring is the peak time for flowers, there are still plenty throughout the summer. Watch out for the following:

Alpenrose: a bright pink member of the rhododendron family which coats the slopes at altitude in June/July.

Viola: a small flower in a variety of colours including yellow, white and blue (or a combination of those colours). It is often found in grassy areas.

Edelweiss: it is the most famous alpine plant, perhaps because it has a song named after it. This rare white flower is striking and hard to spot because it only grows at high altitude (1800–3300m). It prefers limestone's calcareous soils. Look out for it near Cabane FXB Panossière.

Alpenrose
Edelweiss
Joubarbe des Toits
Épilobe des Moraines
Aster des Alpes
Doronic

Waymark near Fenêtre de Durand (Stage 4)

Glaciers & summits of the Combins Massif

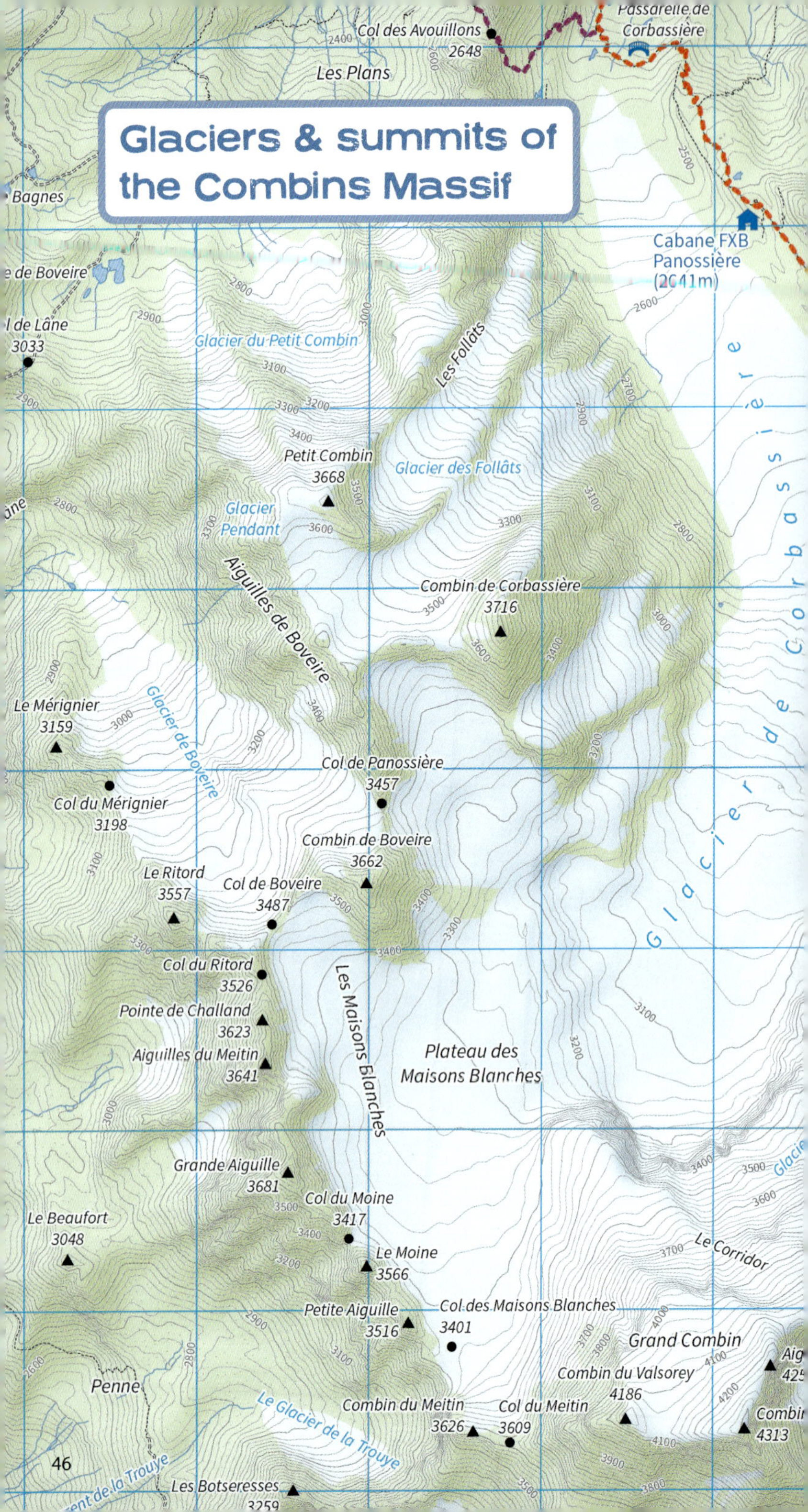

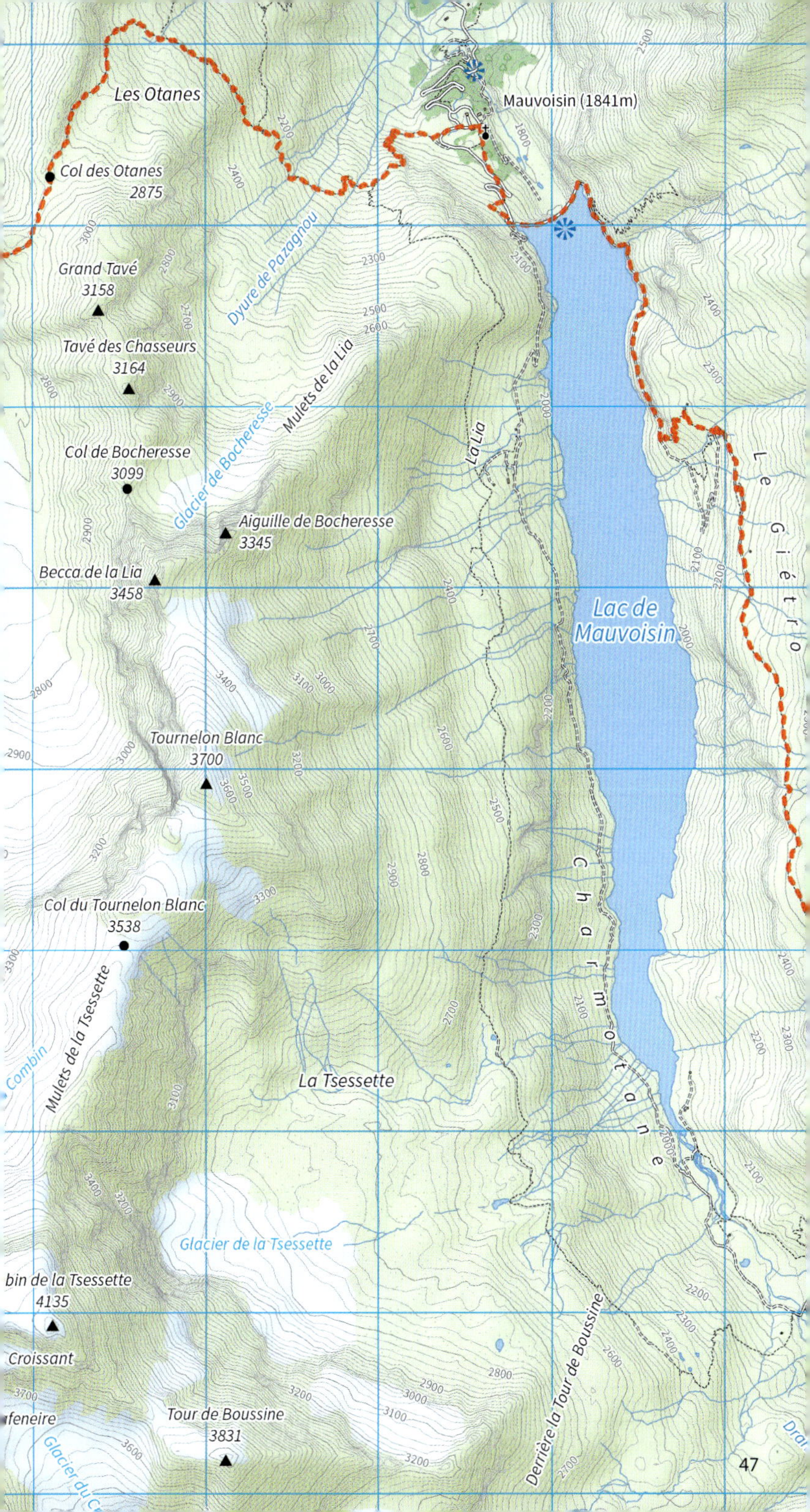
Les Otanes
Mauvoisin (1841m)
Col des Otanes
2875
Grand Tavé
3158
Tavé des Chasseurs
3164
Dyure de Pazagnou
Mulets de la Lia
Glacier de Bocheresse
Col de Bocheresse
3099
Aiguille de Bocheresse
3345
Becca de la Lia
3458
La Lia
Le Giétro
Lac de Mauvoisin
Tournelon Blanc
3700
Col du Tournelon Blanc
3538
Charmotane
Mulets de la Tsessette
Combin
La Tsessette
Glacier de la Tsessette
bin de la Tsessette
4135
Croissant
feneire
Glacier du C
Tour de Boussine
3831
Derrière la Tour de Boussine

1 Bourg-St-Pierre/ Cabane de Mille

Most trekkers start and finish the TDC at BSP which is located along the road that connects Martigny with the Italian town of Aosta (via Col du GSB). For CW trekkers, the route begins with a long climb along the W side of the GC Massif to the mountain hut at Col de Mille. Immediately upon departure from the village of BSP, the path starts upwards and it barely relents until the end: there is no gentle warm up on this trek to give the legs time to adjust to the rigours of long-distance hiking. The good news is that, although the route heads consistently upwards, rarely is the gradient particularly steep, facilitating a comfortable, steady pace. Furthermore, from the outset until the finish, the scenery is exquisite: classic alpine terrain of jagged peaks, deep green valleys and flower-filled pastures grazed by herds of the miraculously pristine cows that seem only to exist in Switzerland.

Stage 1 is much easier for ACW trekkers, on the other hand, who enjoy a straightforward descent from Cabane de Mille to BSP where many people finish the trek: the fabulous scenery ensures an epic climax to an incredible trek.

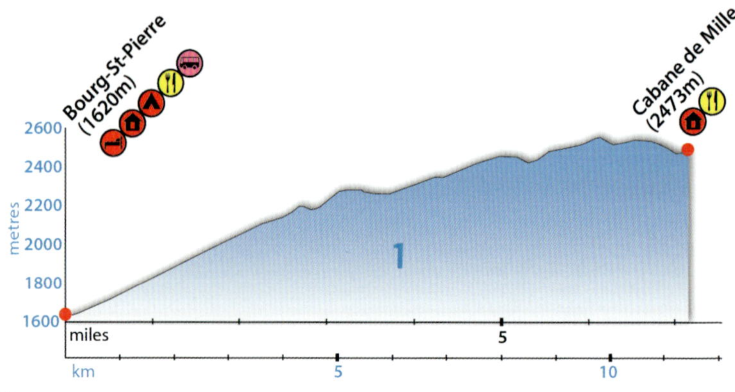

Petit Combin, Grand Combin de Grafeneire & Mont Vélan seen from Cabane de Mille

Accommodation locations: **BSP** has a few hotels, restaurants and a campsite. However, it has no supermarket and there is only a small shop beside the service station (which sells drinks and snacks): stock up on supplies before reaching BSP. Buses travel regularly to BSP from Orsières which is further down the valley: Orsières is linked by rail to the rest of Switzerland.

Cabane de Mille is a modern mountain hut with a spectacular location on Col de Mille: it was rebuilt completely in 2013/2014. It is a comfortable hut with 59 beds in 7 dormitories but can feel a little crowded in high season. The views from the dining room are stunning. To the S, the Combin de Grafeneire (the highest summit in the GC Massif) rises above a dramatic ridge, drawing the eye. However, to its right and slightly further away, the jagged summit of Mont Vélan is even more beautiful. Both mountains look particularly fine at sunset when the alpenglow lights up their snowy faces. To the W, the Mont Blanc Massif is only a stone's throw away: the Grande Jorasses, Mont Dolent and l'Aiguille d'Argentière look magnificent and it hardly matters that you cannot see Mont Blanc itself from here. If you are arriving at the hut early, bring surplus drinking water because taps are sometimes shut off during the day (due to water shortages): they are switched on again in the evening.

Trail conditions: paths and tracks are clear, well maintained and straightforward to negotiate.

Route-finding: straightforward in good conditions. Most significant junctions have signposts/waymarks.

		Time	Distance	Ascent CW	Descent CW
Stage 1	Bourg-St-Pierre/ Cabane de Mille	5:00(CW) 3:45(ACW)	11.4km 7.1miles	1071m 3514ft	218m 715ft

Accommodation

- **BSP (Stage 1/6/v6):** hotels; dormitory beds at Hotel du Crêt
- **Cabane de Mille (Stage 1/2a)**

Camping

- **BSP (Stage 1/6/v6):** Camping Grand Saint Bernard
- **Cabane de Mille (Stage 1/2a):** camping sometimes permitted beside the cabane

Refreshments/Food

- **BSP (Stage 1/6/v6):** restaurants
- **Cabane de Mille (Stage 1/2a)**

Supplies

- **BSP (Stage 1/6/v6):** small shop beside the service station (snacks/drinks)

Escape/Access

- **BSP (Stage 1/6/v6):** bus 210 to/from Orsières and Col du GSB; TMR bus 12.211 to Aosta through the GSB Tunnel (avoiding Col du GSB)

The Mont Blanc Massif viewed from Cabane de Mille

CW

Stage 1: Bourg-St-Pierre to Cabane de Mille

S From the centre of **BSP**, head N on **Rue du Bourg**. TR at a fork and head NE on **Route de la Chapelle/Route Vieille**. Soon, pass under the main road. Shortly afterwards, pass **Hotel Bivouac Napoleon**, a service station and a small shop. Follow a lane climbing N.

1 1:15: At **le Creux du Mâ**, keep SH at a junction: there is a fountain here. Pass in front of a little farm.

2 1:40: TL at a junction. 5min later, TL and cross a stream.

3 2:05: At **Bovière d'en Bas (2200m)**, TL onto a path ('Col de Mille') and contour around the slopes (red/white waymarks).

4 2:35: TR at a junction at a farm, starting to climb again.

5 3:35: Just before **la Vuardette (a small summit; 2462m)**, TR and descend NE across the slopes. Bear left across a small plateau. Then contour NW across the slopes.

F 5:00: Immediately after **Col de Mille (2471m)**, reach **Cabane de Mille (2473m)**.

ACW

Stage 1: Cabane de Mille to Bourg-St-Pierre

F From **Cabane de Mille**, head E to nearby **Col de Mille (2471m)**. Then climb briefly SE: ignore the path climbing E. Contour SE across the face of the slope. From a plateau, descend SW. Soon, start to climb SW.

5 1:20: TL at **la Vuardette (a small summit; 2462m)** and descend SE.

4 1:50: TL at a junction at a farm, heading SE across the slopes.

3 2:10: At **Bovière d'en Bas (2200m)**, TR at a junction ('Bourg-St-Pierre').

2 2:25: 5min after crossing a stream, TR and descend.

1 2:40: At **le Creux du Mâ**, pass in front of a little farm. Just afterwards, keep SH and descend S. Keep SH past **Hotel Bivouac Napoleon** (where there is a service station and a small shop). Shortly afterwards, pass under the main road. Head S on **Route de la Chapelle/Route Vieille**.

S 3:45: TL at a junction and head S on **Rue du Bourg** to enter **BSP (1620m)**.

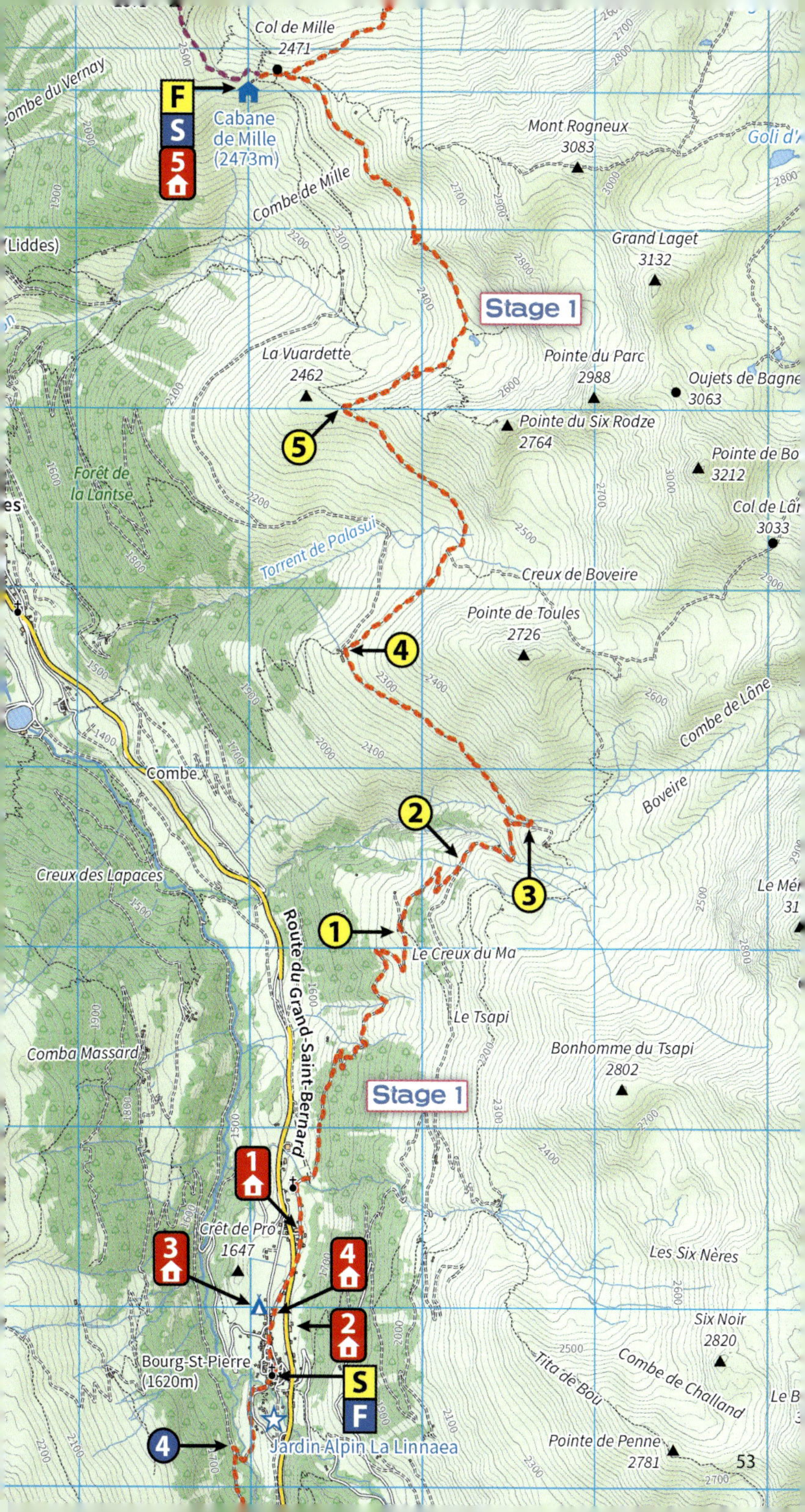

Col de Mille
2471
Cabane de Mille (2473m)
Combe du Vernay
Mont Rogneux
3083
Combe de Mille
(Liddes)
Grand Laget
3132
Stage 1
La Vuardette
2462
Pointe du Parc
2988
Oujets de Bagne
3063
Pointe du Six Rodze
2764
Forêt de la Lantse
Col de Lân
3033
Torrent de Palasui
Creux de Boveire
Pointe de Toules
2726
Combe de Lâne
Combe
Boveire
Creux des Lapaces
Route du Grand-Saint-Bernard
Le Creux du Ma
Le Tsapi
Bonhomme du Tsapi
2802
Comba Massard
Stage 1
Crêt de Pro
1647
Les Six Nères
Six Noir
2820
Bourg-St-Pierre (1620m)
Combe de Challand
Tita de Boû
Jardin Alpin La Linnaea
Pointe de Penne
2781

Orsières/ Cabane de Mille

Many trekkers travel to the region by public transport, taking a train to Orsières and then catching a bus from Orsières to BSP (where the official Stage 1 begins). However, using our Stage v1, it is also possible to start the trek at Orsières, avoiding the need to travel by bus to BSP. Although this is not an official TDC variant, it is just as spectacular as the official Stage 1. Good paths and tracks climb E onto a ridge above the village and then lead you S along it, across the summit of Mont Brûlé, towards Cabane de Mille. The only downside for CW trekkers is that Orsières sits at a significantly lower altitude than BSP and consequently, hiking from Orsières entails 600m more climbing than if you begin at BSP. This means that Stage v1 is significantly harder than Stage 1.

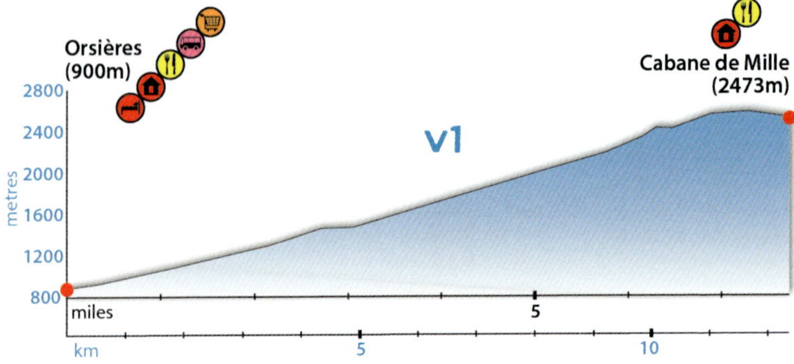

Mont Fort seen from Mont Brûlé

Stage v1 is an easier proposition for ACW trekkers who simply descend from Cabane de Mille to Orsières, finishing the trek there rather than BSP. This avoids the need to take a bus from BSP to Orsières station at the end of the trek.

Accommodation locations: **Orsières** has a good hotel, restaurants and supermarkets. It is linked by rail to the rest of Switzerland.

Cabane de Mille: see p49.

Trail conditions: paths and tracks are clear, well maintained and straightforward to negotiate.

Route-finding: Between S and 3, there is a complicated labyrinth of paths, tracks and minor roads: follow waymarks and signs carefully. Otherwise, route-finding is largely straightforward in good conditions: most significant junctions have signposts/waymarks. Between 5 and Cabane de Mille, the route uses the crest of a ridge which you should avoid in high winds, low visibility or snowy conditions.

		Time	Distance	Ascent CW	Descent CW
Stage v1	Orsières/ Cabane de Mille	6:00(CW) 4:00(ACW)	12.5km 7.8miles	1689m 5542ft	116m 381ft

Accommodation

- **Orsières (Stage v1):** hotel (private rooms; dormitory)
- **Cabane de Mille (Stage 1/v1/2a)**

Camping

- **Cabane de Mille (Stage 1/v1/2a):** camping sometimes permitted beside the cabane

Refreshments/Food

- **Orsières (Stage v1):** restaurants; bars
- **Cabane de Mille (Stage 1/v1/2a)**

Supplies

- **Orsières (Stage v1):** supermarkets; outdoor store; shops; ATM

Escape/Access

- **Orsières (Stage v1):** trains to Sembrancher, le Châble and Martigny;
  Bus 210 to/from BSP and Col du GSB;
  TMR bus 12.211 to Aosta through the GSB Tunnel (avoiding Col du GSB)

Cabane de Mille

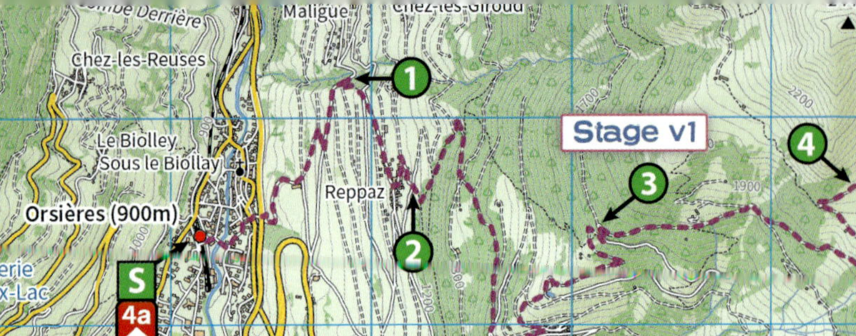

CW

Stage v1: Orsières to Cabane de Mille

S From **Orsières station**, head E down **Rue du Châtelard**. Shortly afterwards, descend steps. Then cross a bridge over the river. Shortly afterwards, TL on a road. Soon, TR and climb on a path between houses. Shortly afterwards, keep SH across a road. Now the route climbs using a combination of roads, tracks and paths (yellow/black waymarks).

1 0:30: TR onto a track. Shortly afterwards, TL onto a path (easy to miss). Soon, TR and climb on a road: ignore a smaller track on the right which descends. TL in the hamlet of **Reppaz** and climb between buildings. Shortly afterwards, follow the road around to the right.

2 1:00: Shortly, at a junction, TL onto a path which soon climbs through forest ('Commeire'). At times, the route is unclear and not every junction is marked. When you reach a road, follow it up through **Commeire**.

3 2:45: TR at a junction and climb on a track ('les Planards').

4 4:15: TL onto a narrow path (easy to miss; 'Cabane de Mille').

5 5:15: Keep SH at a junction. Eventually, the path leads you along the top of the ridge: keep SH across **Mont Brûlé (2571m)**.

F 6:00: Arrive at **Cabane de Mille (2473m)**.

ACW

Stage v1: Cabane de Mille to Orsières

F From **Cabane de Mille**, climb on a path which heads initially W: soon bear right to head N. Keep SH across **Mont Brûlé (2571m)**. Then descend N along a ridge.

5 0:30: Bear left at a junction and descend NW on a path.

4 1:05: TR and descend on a track.

3 2:00: TL at a junction and continue descending on a track. When you reach a road, follow it down through **Commeire**. Soon leave the road for a track on the left: descend through forest. At times, the route is unclear: not every junction is marked.

2 3:05: Keep SH onto a road which descends through the hamlet of **Reppaz**. At a junction on the W side of the village, TR and head N on a road. 10min later, TL and descend on a steep path.

1 3:30: TR onto a track. Shortly afterwards, TL down a road. Now the route descends using a combination of roads, tracks and paths (yellow/black waymarks). Later, keep SH across a road and descend on a path between houses. Shortly afterwards, TL along another road. A few minutes later, TR and cross a bridge over the river. Climb steps and then TL up **Rue du Châtelard**.

S 4:00: Shortly afterwards, reach **Orsières station (900m)**.

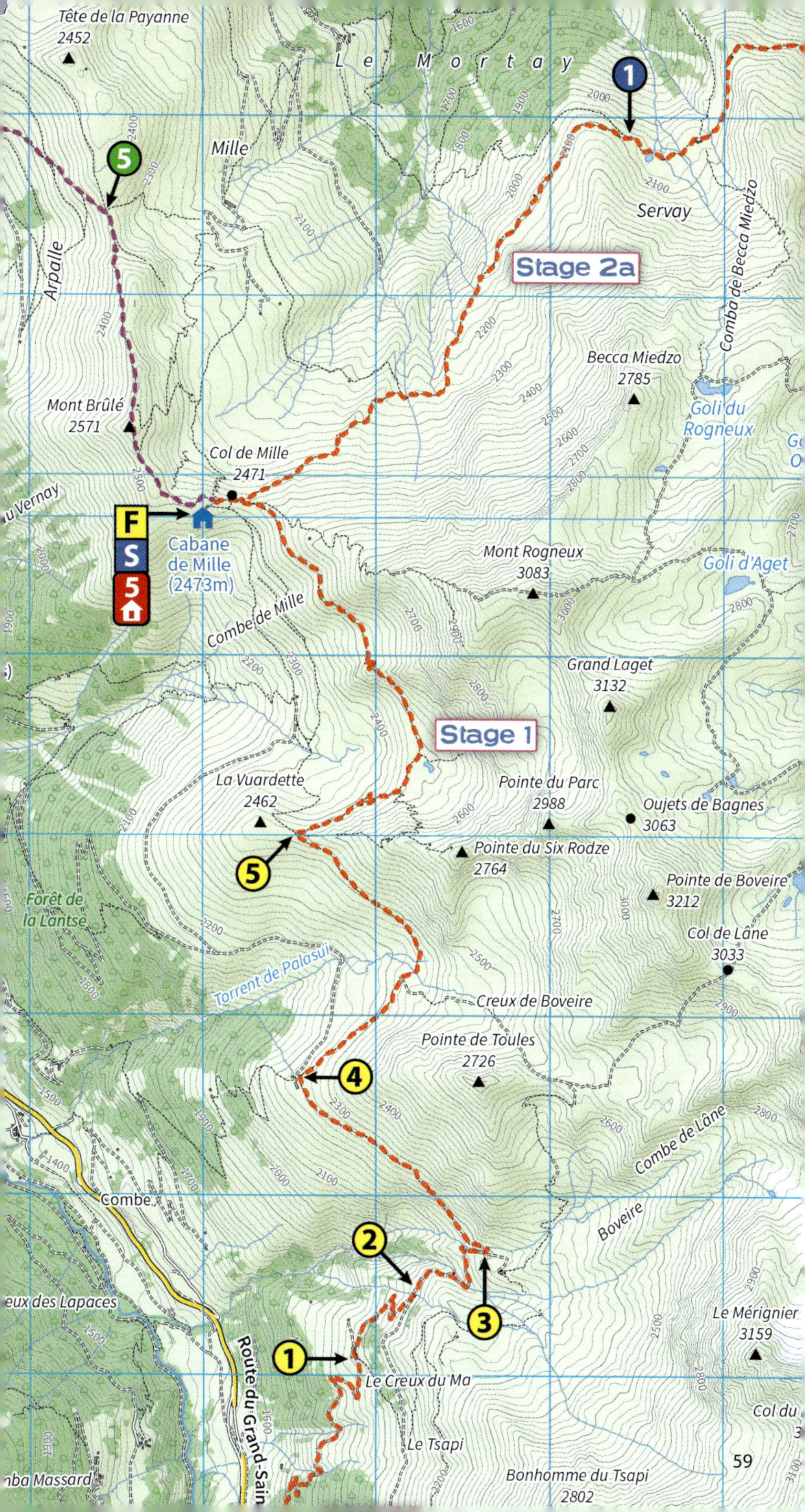

Tête de la Payanne
2452
Le Mortay
Mille
Servay
Comba de Becca Miedzo
Stage 2a
Arpaille
Becca Miedzo
2785
Goli du
Rogneux
Mont Brûlé
2571
Col de Mille
2471
Cabane
de Mille
(2473m)
Mont Rogneux
3083
Goli d'Aget
Combe de Mille
Grand Laget
3132
Stage 1
La Vuardette
2462
Pointe du Parc
2988
Oujets de Bagnes
3063
Pointe du Six Rodze
2764
Pointe de Boveire
3212
Forêt de
la Lantse
Col de Lâne
3033
Torrent de Palasui
Creux de Boveire
Pointe de Toules
2726
Combe de Lâne
Combe
Boveire
Le Mérignier
3159
Le Creux du Ma
Route du Grand-Sain
Le Tsapi
Bonhomme du Tsapi
2802

2 Cabane de Mille/ Cabane FXB Panossière

Although the route of Section 2 undulates regularly, it never dips below 2000m, ensuring that you retain most of the altitude gained on the previous day (irrespective of direction of travel) and therefore enjoy views of the highest quality throughout. Scenically, this spectacular section can be split into two parts: Stage 2a travels a fabulous balcony path along the N side of the GC Massif, overlooking the lovely Val de Bagnes. However, the second part (Stage 2b) is even more beautiful, exploring the interior of the massif, further away from civilisation. At the N end of Stage 2b, there are great views of the Petit Combin but closer to Cabane FXB Panossière, Grand Combin de Grafeneire (the highest summit in the massif) dominates. In our opinion, Stage 2b is more spectacular if travelled in a CW direction because you face the high summits and, as you reach Cabane FXB Panossière, the sudden appearance of the Glacier de Corbassière is awe-inspiring.

Accommodation locations: at each end of the route, there is a wonderfully situated mountain hut: CW trekkers will already have experienced **Cabane de Mille** which is superbly positioned at the W end of Section 2 (see p49).

At the E end, **Cabane FXB Panossière** sits on a promontory just above the lateral moraine of the Corbassière Glacier: it overlooks the glacier and Grand Combin de

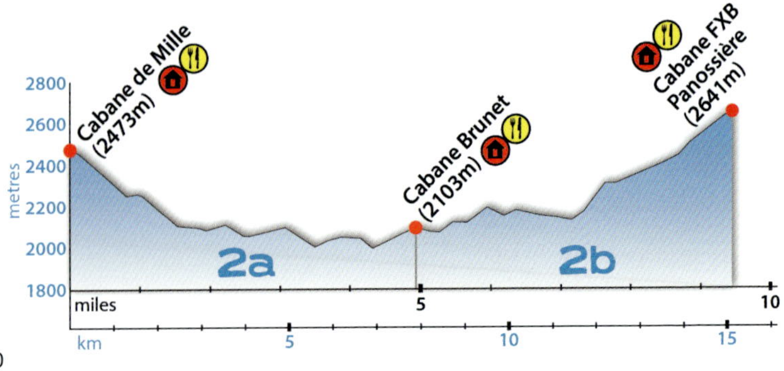

Cabane FXB Panossière

Grafeneire. It provides arguably the finest panorama on the entire trek and is an extremely popular location: book in advance. It is a comfortable hut with 75 beds. The current structure was built in 1996 and is the fifth refuge to have been built on the site: the first one was constructed in 1881. The dining room has beautiful views but the outside terrace is mind-blowing.

A third hut, **Cabane Brunet**, is located half-way along Section 2 which means that you can split this part of the trek into two shorter days. It was built in 1942 and has 56 dormitory places. It is a lovely place but can be quite busy during the day. You can see Petit Combin from the terrace.

Trail conditions: paths and tracks are clear, well maintained and straightforward to negotiate. However, on Stage 2b between 2 and 3, the path can be hard to follow over sections of rocks: watch carefully for waymarks. This section of the route also crosses Passarelle de Corbassière, a suspension bridge over a deep gorge: the bridge is modern but those with a fear of heights might find it to be a challenge.

Route-finding: straightforward in good conditions, except between 2 and 3 on Stage 2b (see above). Most significant junctions have signposts/waymarks. Sometimes, snow can remain on the highest sections of the route into July, making navigation more difficult.

		Time	Distance	Ascent CW	Descent CW
Stage 2a	Cabane de Mille/ Cabane Brunet	3:00(CW) 3:45(ACW)	7.9km 4.9miles	340m 1116ft	710m 2330ft
Stage 2b	Cabane Brunet/ Cabane FXB Panossière	3:30(CW) 2:30(ACW)	7.2km 4.5miles	729m 2392ft	191m 627ft

Accommodation

- Cabane de Mille (Stage 1/2a)
- Cabane Brunet (Stage 2a/2b)
- Cabane FXB Panossière (Stage 2b/3a)

Camping

- **Cabane de Mille (Stage 1/2a):** camping sometimes permitted beside the cabane

Grand Combin de Grafeneire (the highest summit in the massif)

Refreshments/Food

- Cabane de Mille (Stage 1/2a)
- Cabane Brunet (Stage 2a/2b)
- Cabane FXB Panossière (Stage 2b/3a)

Supplies

- None

Escape/Access

- **Cabane Brunet (Stage 2a/2b):** from the cabane, a path descends N into the valley to the buildings at la Barmasse. From there, descend NW to the road where there is a bus stop at a hairpin bend (see map). Postbus 253 heads NW down Val de Bagnes to the train station at le Châble: there are trains to Orsières and Martigny (both via Sembrancher). Postbus 253 also heads up the valley to Mauvoisin (Stage 3a/3b)

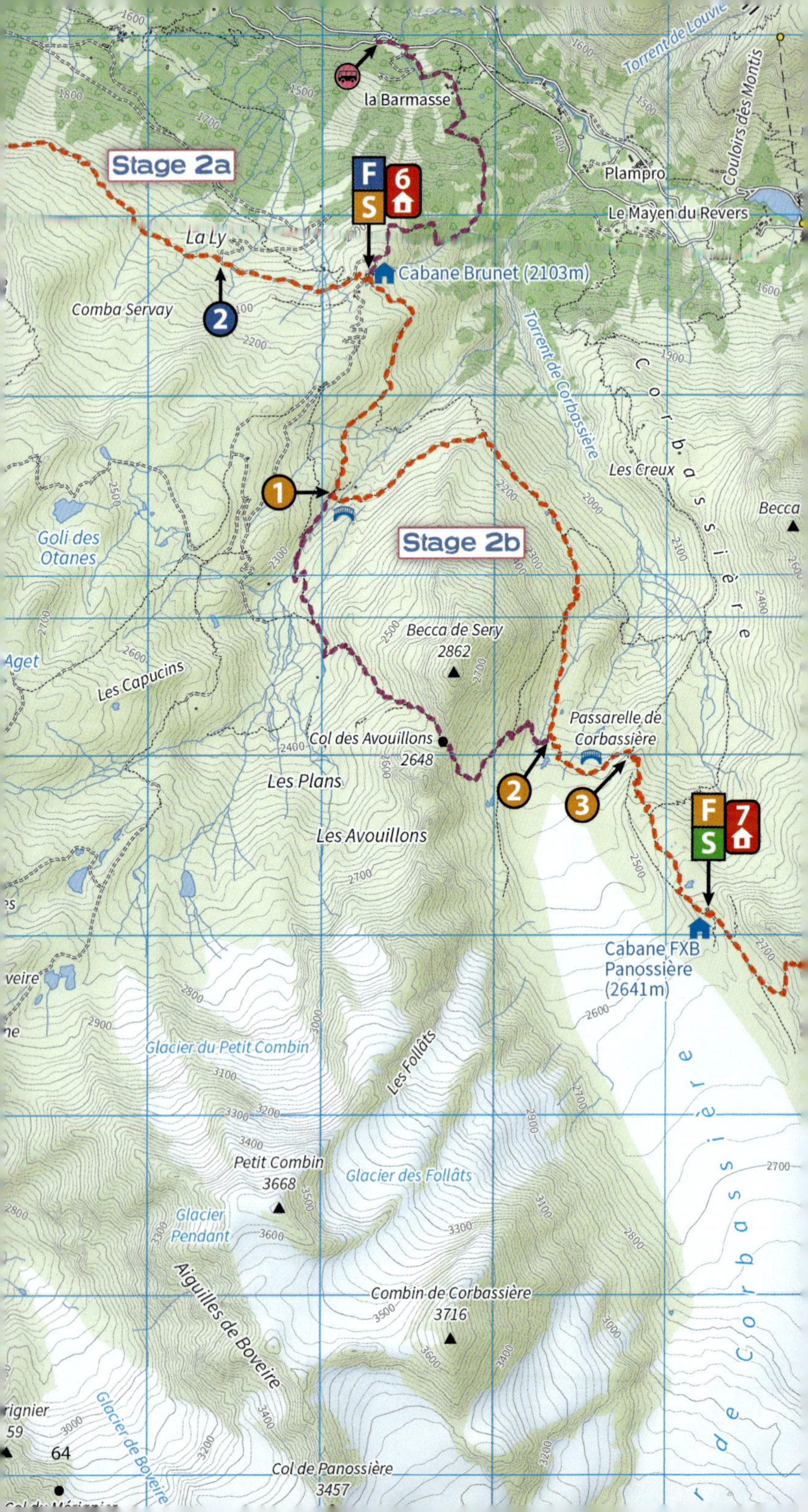

Stage 2a
Stage 2b
la Barmasse
Plampro
Le Mayen du Revers
Torrent de Louvie
Couloirs des Montis
La Ly
Comba Servay
Cabane Brunet (2103m)
Torrent de Corbassière
Les Creux
Becca
Goli des Otanes
Aget
Les Capucins
Becca de Sery
2862
Col des Avouillons
2648
Les Plans
Les Avouillons
Passarelle de Corbassière
Cabane FXB Panossière (2641m)
Glacier du Petit Combin
Les Follâts
Petit Combin
3668
Glacier des Follâts
Glacier Pendant
Aiguilles de Boveire
Combin de Corbassière
3716
Glacier de Boveire
Col de Panossière
3457
64

The Giétro Glacier Disaster

Perched high above Val de Bagnes, the 4.5km long Glacier du Giétro is fed by snowfall on the slopes of Mont Blanc de Cheilon. Today, the outflow from the glacier drains into Lac de Mauvoisin where it is held captive by the walls of the Barrage de Mauvoisin. Prior to the construction of the dam, however, the water was free to flow into the river Dranse de Bagnes and make its way unimpeded down the valley towards Martigny. In 1816, seracs falling from the terminus of the glacier gradually formed a natural dam of ice in the valley (150m high) which blocked the flow of the Dranse de Bagnes and created a huge lake (2km long and 60m deep). On 16 June 1818, the ice dam gave way and 18 million m^3 of water charged down the valley. Within 30min, it had ravaged the entire valley, even causing significant damage in Martigny. 44 people were killed. In fact, the disaster could have been even worse because, in the weeks beforehand, engineers had drained some of the water from the lake by drilling holes in the ice.

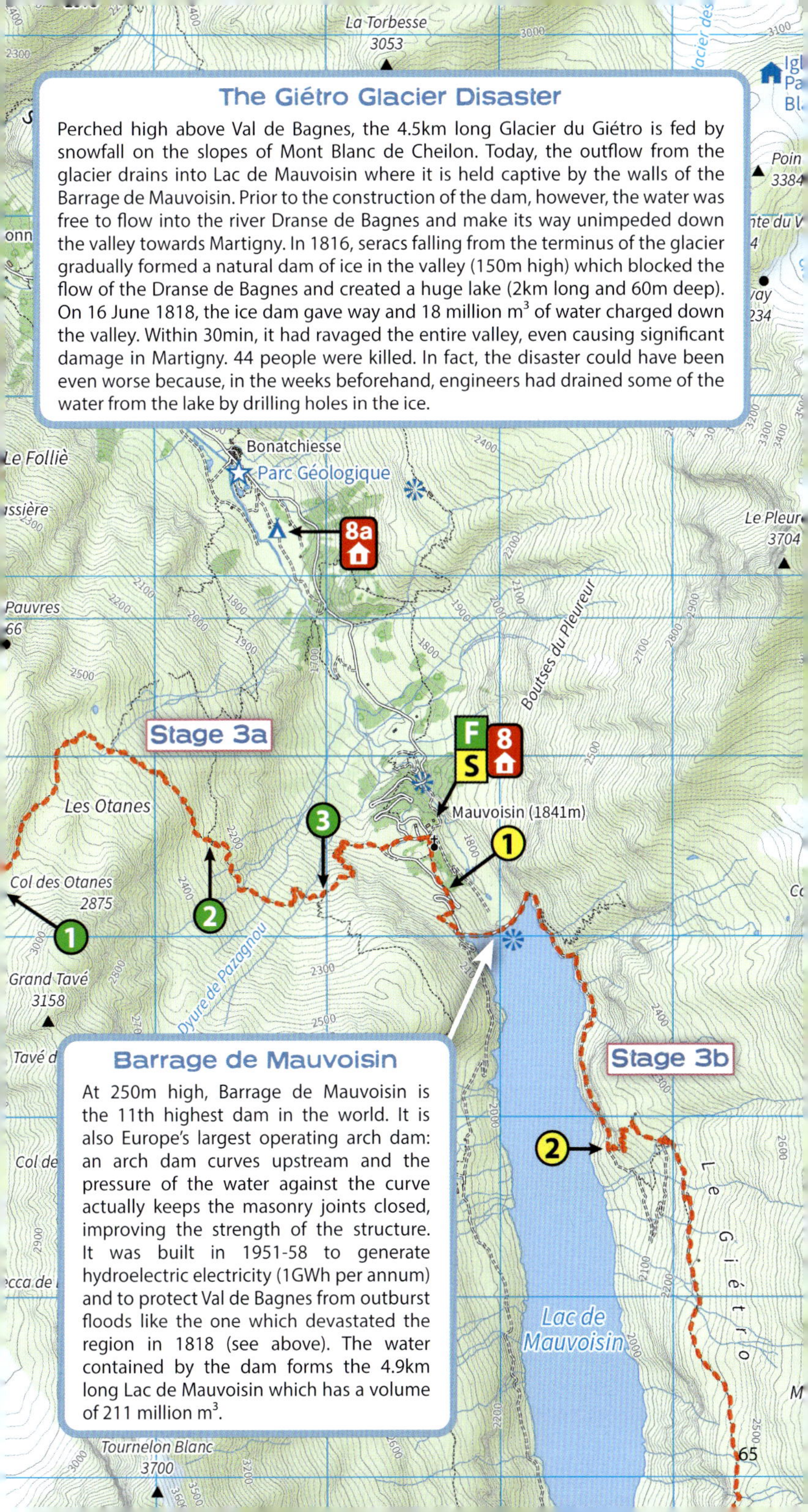

Stage 3a

Stage 3b

Barrage de Mauvoisin

At 250m high, Barrage de Mauvoisin is the 11th highest dam in the world. It is also Europe's largest operating arch dam: an arch dam curves upstream and the pressure of the water against the curve actually keeps the masonry joints closed, improving the strength of the structure. It was built in 1951-58 to generate hydroelectric electricity (1GWh per annum) and to protect Val de Bagnes from outburst floods like the one which devastated the region in 1818 (see above). The water contained by the dam forms the 4.9km long Lac de Mauvoisin which has a volume of 211 million m^3.

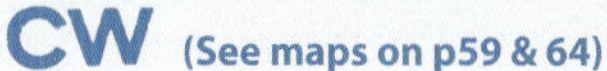

CW (See maps on p59 & 64)

Stage 2a: Cabane de Mille to Cabane Brunet

S From **Cabane de Mille**, head E to nearby **Col de Mille (2471m)**. Cross the col and descend NE on a path which contours around the slopes.

1 1:20: Keep SH at a junction, descending towards a small lake. Continue E past the lake: there are trout in the clear water. Shortly afterwards, keep SH past the farm buildings of **Servay**, ignoring any paths to the left which descend into the valley. An undulating path continues contouring around the slopes.

2 2:40: Keep SH up a track. 15min later, TR and climb on a path.

F 3:00: Arrive at **Cabane Brunet (2103m)**.

Stage 2b: Cabane Brunet to Cabane FXB Panossière

S From **Cabane Brunet**, head initially SE on a path which contours around the slopes. Soon, the path bends right and heads S: there are great views of **Becca de Sery** and **Petit Combin**.

1 0:40: TL at a junction and descend: alternatively, keep SH for a variant high route via **Col des Avouillons**. Shortly afterwards cross a suspension bridge over the **Dyure de Sery**. Then contour around the slopes of **Becca de Sery**: on the E side of it, the path zigzags steeply upwards to the S.

2 2:20: TL at a junction: the alternative high route via Col des Avouillons joins from the right. Now follow red/white waymarks across rocky terrain: there are short sections of rocks to climb and markings are sometimes hard to follow. A few minutes later, cross **Passarelle de Corbassière**, a huge suspension bridge. Afterwards, TL and climb on a rocky path.

3 2:45: TR at a junction and climb a steep ridge. Further up, there are edelweiss beside the path.

F 3:30: Arrive at **Cabane FXB Panossière (2641m)**.

ACW (See maps on p64 & 59)

Stage 2b: Cabane FXB Panossière to Cabane Brunet

F From **Cabane FXB Panossière**, descend NW along the crest of a ridge: look out for edelweiss beside the path.

3 0:30: TL at a junction, heading W on a rocky path. 10min later, cross **Passarelle de Corbassière**, a huge suspension bridge. Now follow red/white waymarks across rocky terrain: there are short sections of rocks to descend and markings are sometimes hard to follow.

2 0:50: TR at a junction: alternatively, TL for a variant high route via **Col des Avouillons**. The magnificent path now heads along the E flank of **Becca de Sery**. Soon zigzag steeply downwards to the N. Then the path bends left and heads around the N flank of **Becca de Sery**. At the NW side of **Becca de Sery**, cross a suspension bridge over the **Dyure de Sery** and climb briefly.

1 2:00: TR at a junction, heading N: the alternative high route via Col des Avouillons joins from the left. After a while, the path bends left and heads NW.

S 2:30: Shortly afterwards, reach **Cabane Brunet (2103m)**.

Stage 2a: Cabane Brunet to Cabane de Mille

F From **Cabane Brunet**, descend W on a path. After a few minutes, TL down a track.

2 0:15: TL onto a path which soon contours around the slopes to the W. About 75min later, keep SH past the farm buildings of **Servay**, ignoring any paths to the right which descend into the valley. Continue W past the lake: there are trout in the clear water.

1 1:40: Keep left at a junction, ignoring a path to the right which descends into the valley. Contour around the slopes again. Soon the path bends left and climbs SW.

S 3:45: Climb across **Col de Mille (2471m)**. Keep SH to reach nearby **Cabane de Mille (2473m)**.

Val de Bagnes
(Stage 2a)

3 Cabane FXB Panossière/ Cabane de Chanrion

This is the most remote part of the TDC and the variety and quality of the landscapes on display are staggering. It hardly seems possible but the views of the Corbassière Glacier and Grand Combin de Grafeneire are even better as you climb to Col des Otanes than at Panossière. And from up there, Petit Combin and Combin de Corbassière (to the SW) look incredible, particularly at sunrise: we highly recommend an early start from Panossière for CW trekkers. After such superlative scenes, CW trekkers may find that the broad flat col itself is slightly anticlimactic but do not worry because the jaw-dropping views soon return as you descend E to Mauvoisin through a wonderland of waterfalls and greenery. Watch for ibex and chamois on both sides of the col.

At Mauvoisin (which sits on the floor of Val de Bagnes), the TDC has something unique to offer because it uses a tunnel through the hillside to climb to the top of Barrage de Mauvoisin, Europe's largest operating arch dam (see p65). It then leads you over the dam wall and up the slopes on the E side of the stunning turquoise Lac de Mauvoisin. A good path then travels the wild terrain along the E side of the GC Massif to Cabane de Chanrion (which is one of the most isolated huts in Europe).

Accommodation locations: at each end of the route, there is a wonderfully situated mountain hut: CW trekkers will already have experienced **Cabane FXB Panossière** which lies at the W end of Section 3 (see p60).

The lovely **Cabane de Chanrion**, at the E end, is one of our favourite huts in the Alps. The original hut at this site was built in 1890. The current structure is a lovely marriage of old and new: the older stone building dates from 1938 and the modern structure

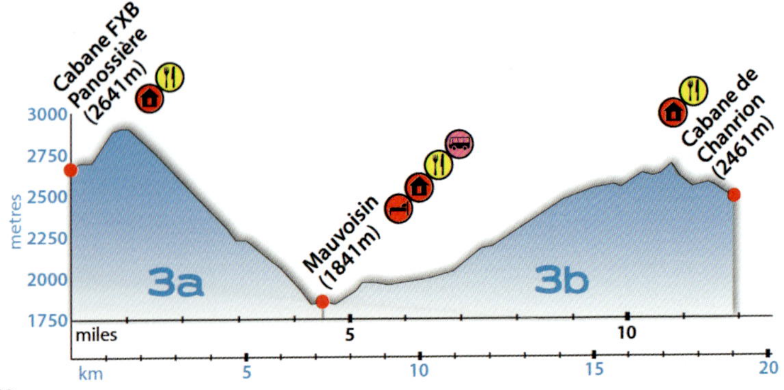

Combin de la Tsessette

was completed in 2022. The gardiens are welcoming and the food is as good as you will find in a Swiss alpine hut.

If you feel like stopping mid-section, there is a hotel at **Mauvoisin** which dates back more than 150 years. It has a nice location but bear in mind that Val de Bagnes is steep-sided here and the sun arrives late in the morning and leaves early in the evening.

Trail conditions: the trail between Cabane FXB Panossière and Col des Otanes is very steep. On both sides of the col, the paths are rocky and uneven: take care. The route between the col and Mauvoisin is long and steep: for CW trekkers, the descent is tough on the knees and for ACW trekkers, it is a brutal climb. This section also has chains and steps on some exposed sections: take care.

At the W side of Mauvoisin Dam, the route uses a tunnel (built during the dam's construction) which leads you up to, or down from, the top of the dam. The tunnel is well lit and quite spacious, however, those with claustrophobia might prefer to avoid it by walking up/down the road instead. The tunnel is decorated with fascinating photographs taken during the construction of the dam. There are more dark tunnels on the E side of the dam: unfortunately, there is no way of avoiding them. Between the dam and Col de Tsofeiret, the path is largely clear, well-maintained and straightforward to walk upon. However, the trail immediately S of Col de Tsofeiret is steep and unstable: take care.

Route-finding: Section 3 involves the crossing of remote and challenging high mountain terrain. In good conditions, navigation is largely straightforward. However, in poor conditions or low visibility, navigation on certain sections can be tricky. Follow waymarks carefully through the flat wasteland near Col des Otanes because the path can be hard to follow over the rocks: navigation can be tricky here in low visibility. Furthermore, snow can remain near the col into July, making navigation more difficult: red/white posts have been strategically placed to assist. If in doubt, seek the advice of the hut managers at Panossière/Chanrion before setting out.

		Time	Distance	Ascent CW	Descent CW
Stage 3a	Cabane FXB Panossière/ Mauvoisin	3:00(CW) 4:30(ACW)	7.3km 4.5miles	288m 945ft	1088m 3750ft
Stage 3b	Mauvoisin/ Cabane de Chanrion	5:00(CW) 4:00(ACW)	11.6km 7.2miles	989m 3245ft	369m 1211ft

Accommodation

- **Cabane FXB Panossière (Stage 2b/3a)**
- **Hotel de Mauvoisin (Stage 3a/3b):** private rooms; dormitory beds
- **Cabane de Chanrion (Stage 3b/4)**

Camping

- **La Forêt de Mélèzes campsite:** 1.7km OR from Mauvoisin

Refreshments/Food

- **Cabane FXB Panossière (Stage 2b/3a)**
- **Hotel de Mauvoisin (Stage 3a/3b)**
- **Cabane de Chanrion (Stage 3b/4)**

Supplies

- **None**

Escape/Access

- **Mauvoisin (Stage 3a/3b):** Postbus 253 heads NW down the valley to the train station at le Châble. Trains travel between le Châble and Martigny (via Sembrancher). At Sembrancher, you can also change to the branch line which heads to Orsières

Lac de Mauvoisin

Glacier
Col du Tournelon Blanc
3538
Mulets de la Tsessette
Plateau des
Maisons Blanches
La Tse
Glacier du Grand Combin
Le Corridor
Glacier de la Tsessette
Combin de la Tsessette
4135
Col des Maisons Blanches
3401
Grand Combin
Aiguille du Croissant
4259
Combin du Valsorey
4186
Col du Meitin
3609
3626
Combin de Grafeneire
4313
Tour de Boussine
3831
Glacier du Croissant
Col du Sonadon
3503
Le Glacier du Sonadon
Mont Sonadon
3577
Pic d'Amiante
3563
Grande Tête de By
3587
Sphinx du Valsorey
3431
Col Vert
3392
Col d'Amiante
3307
Les Champignons
3359
Pointe des Luisettes
3444
Aiguille Verte de Valsorey
3490
Tête Blanche de By
3418
Piccola Testa di By
3291
Mont Percé
3353
Col de By
3188
Col du Filon
3255
Grand Carré
3334
Aiguilles de Valsorey
Pointe Farinet
2987
Rifugio Franco
Chiarella all'Amianthe
Le Râteau
3275
Grande Maison - Pointe Sud
3038
Grande Maison -
Pointe Nord
3059
Tête du Filon
3306
Pointe Patti
2871
Brèche des Moleires
3190
Les Trois Frères
3259
Dent
Tza dell'Alpe Comune
Pointe de la Bonne Morte
72

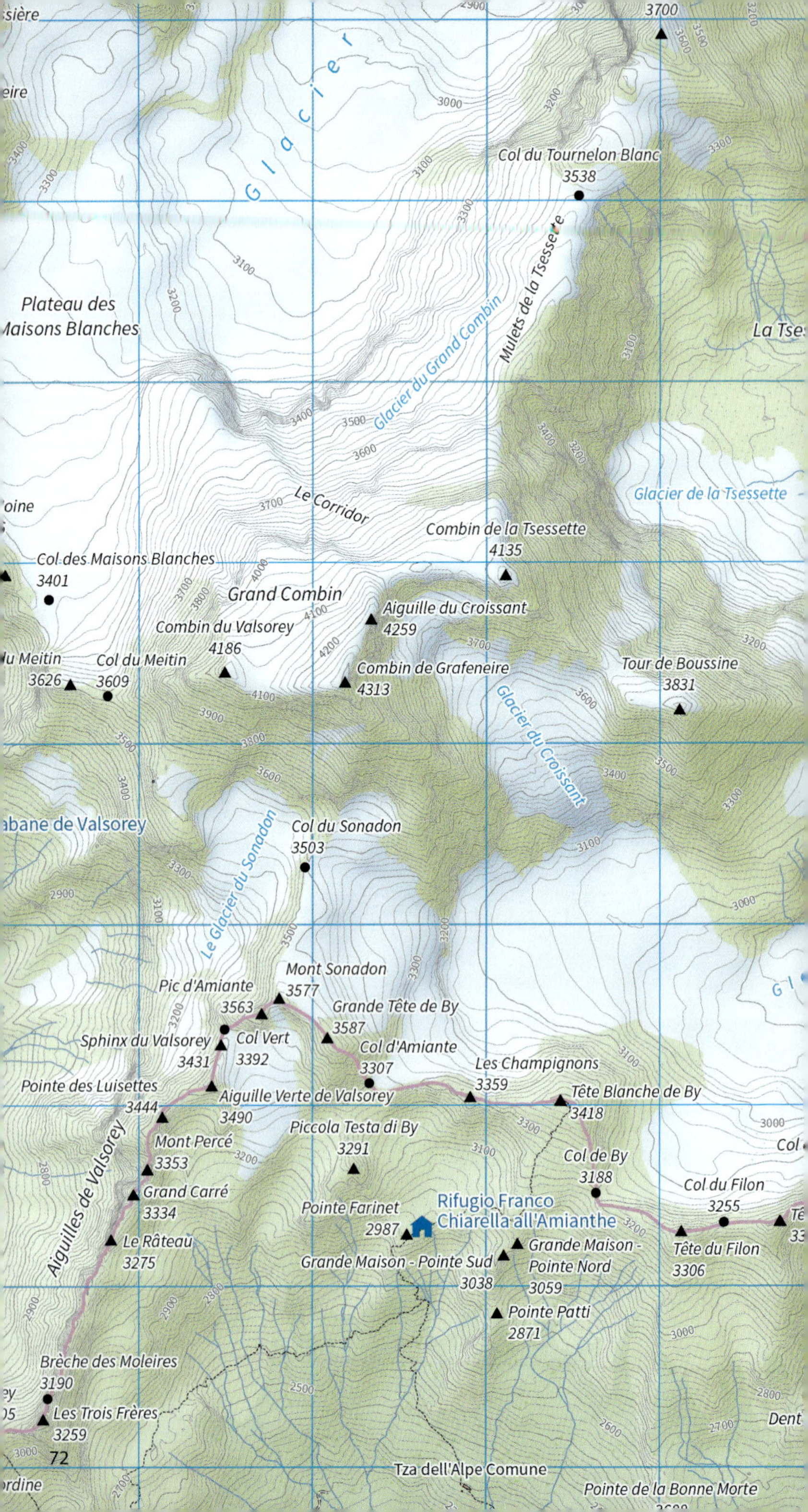

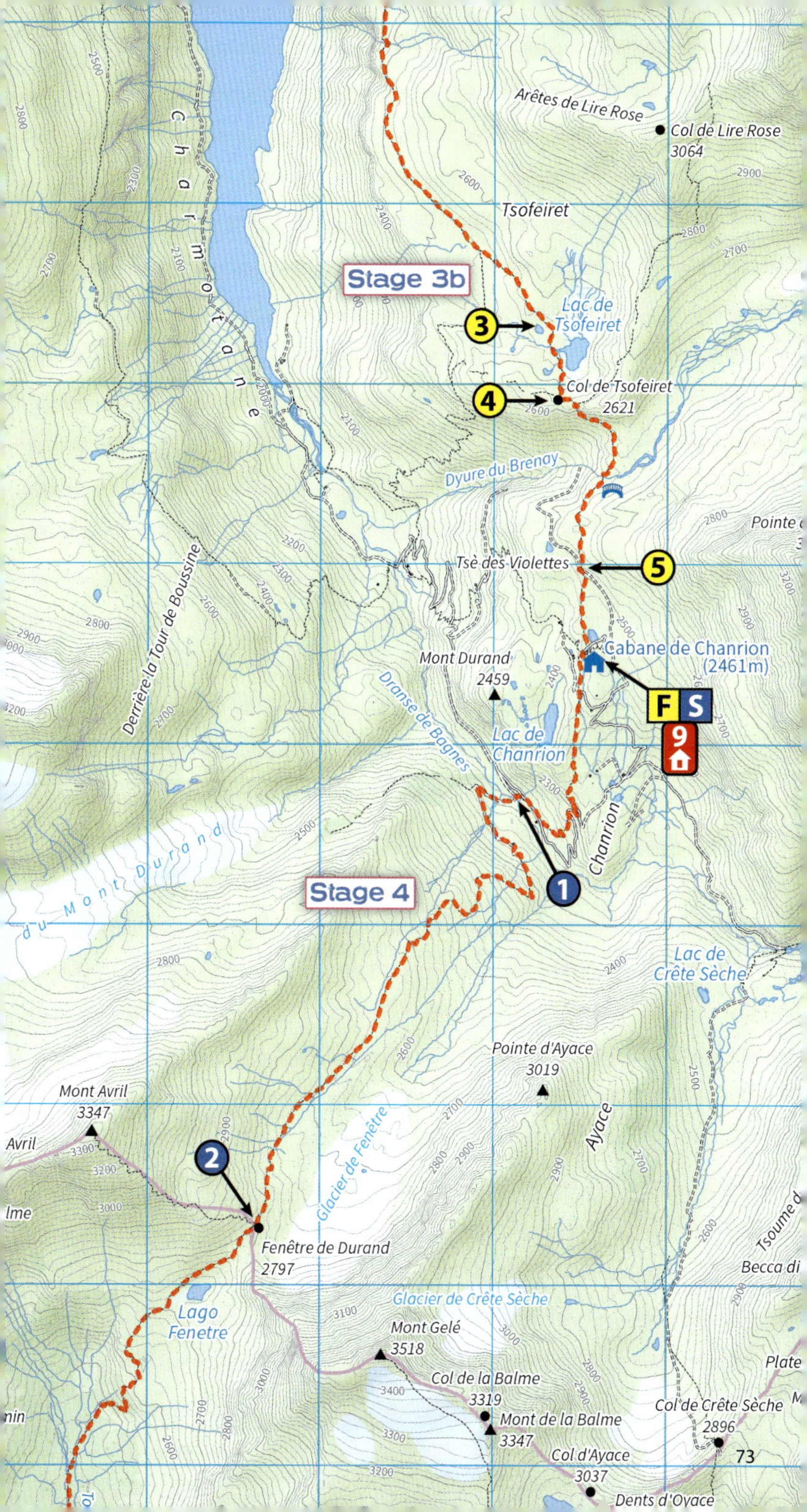
Stage 3b
Stage 4
Arêtes de Lire Rose
Col de Lire Rose
3064
Tsofeiret
Lac de Tsofeiret
Col de Tsofeiret
2621
Dyure du Brenay
Tsè des Violettes
Cabane de Chanrion (2461m)
F
S
9
Mont Durand
2459
Dranse de Bagnes
Lac de Chanrion
Chanrion
Lac de Crête Sèche
Pointe d'Ayace
3019
Ayace
Mont Avril
3347
Fenêtre de Durand
2797
Glacier de Fenêtre
Lago Fenetre
Glacier de Crête Sèche
Mont Gelé
3518
Col de la Balme
3319
Mont de la Balme
3347
Col d'Ayace
3037
Dents d'Oyace
Col de Crête Sèche
2896
Becca di
Derrière la Tour de Boussine
Chanrion
du Mont Durand
Mauvoisin

CW (See maps on p64, 65 & 73)

Stage 3a: Cabane FXB Panossière to Mauvoisin

S From **Cabane FXB Panossière**, head S along the lateral moraine of **Corbassière Glacier**. 10min later, just after a little hut, the path bends left and starts to climb the steep slope to the E. The views are sublime.

1 0:50: Keep SH across **Col des Otanes (2875m)**, following red/white waymarks through a rocky moonscape. This is the TDC's highest point. Soon start to descend: to the E, **Mont Blanc de Cheilon (3870m)** and the **Giétro Glacier** appear. At times, the path is steep and exposed: there are chains and steps to assist. Occasionally, the path disappears at sections of rocks: follow waymarks carefully. After a while, the route bends right and heads SE across the slope.

2 2:15: TR at a junction, still heading SE.

3 2:40: TL at a junction, still descending. Keep SH across a grassy plateau. A few minutes later, TL at a fork (easy to miss) and descend on a path: ignore the grassy track on the right. Soon, keep SH down a road. TR at the next junction.

F 3:00: Just afterwards, reach the hotel at **Mauvoisin (1841m)**.

Stage 3b: Mauvoisin to Cabane de Chanrion

S From the car park beside the hotel, climb S on a path ('Barrage'). Soon, pass a little chapel and a military bunker (built in the 1930s).

1 0:10: Cross a road and enter a pedestrian tunnel (good lighting). Soon, climb steeply. When you exit the tunnel, TL up the road (which goes through another tunnel). A few minutes later, TL at a junction (within the tunnel). Shortly, emerge from the tunnel and head across the top of the dam: the views are wonderful. At the E side of the dam, TR and enter the first of a series of tunnels which head S alongside the lake: it can be quite dark. Eventually, emerge from the final tunnel and continue S along the shore of **Lac de Mauvoisin**.

2 1:20: TL onto a path (easy to miss) and climb steeply E. 15-20min later, TR at some beautiful old farm buildings. Shortly afterwards, cross a stream and then TL up a track. Soon, climb S parallel to the lake: the views across it are spectacular.

3 3:50: Pass a small lake. To the E, **Grand Combin de Grafeneire (4313m)** is just visible behind **Combin de la Tsessette (4135m)**. Soon, cross a stream and pass another lake (**Lac de Tsofeiret**). Afterwards, climb again.

4 4:10: Cross **Col de Tsofeiret (2621m)**. Then take care descending a steep, exposed slope (fixed chains). Cross a section of rocks. Use a bridge to cross to the S side of the **Dyure du Brenay**. Then cross another section of rocks.

5 4:50: Cross a track and descend on a path.

F 5:00: Arrive at **Cabane de Chanrion (2461m)**.

ACW (See maps on p73, 65 & 64)

Stage 3b: Cabane de Chanrion to Mauvoisin

F From **Cabane de Chanrion**, head N on a path.

5 0:10: Keep SH across a track. Cross a section of rocks. Use a bridge to cross to the N side of the **Dyure du Brenay**. Then cross another section of rocks. Take care climbing a steep, exposed slope out of the valley (fixed chains).

4 1:10: Cross **Col de Tsofeiret (2621m)** and descend. Keep SH past **Lac de Tsofeiret (2572m)**. Soon, cross a stream.

3 1:25: Shortly afterwards, pass another smaller lake: to the E, **Grand Combin de Grafeneire (4313m)** is just visible behind **Combin de la Tsessette (4135m)**. Soon, descend N parallel to **Lac de Mauvoisin**: the views across it are spectacular. After a while, keep SH on a track. Later, follow the track downhill to the W: at the third hairpin bend, leave the track and head NW on a path. Shortly afterwards, TL at some beautiful old farm buildings and descend to the W.

2 3:05: TR onto a track and head N along the lake shore. Soon, pass through a series of tunnels which head N alongside the lake. Emerge from the final tunnel and head across the top of the dam: the views are wonderful. At the W side of the dam, follow the road into another tunnel. Shortly afterwards, TR at a junction (within the tunnel). When you exit the tunnel, TR along the road. Shortly afterwards, TR and enter a pedestrian tunnel (good lighting) which leads you down through the hillside.

1 3:55: Emerge from the tunnel and cross the road. Descend N on a path. Soon, pass a military bunker (built in the 1930s) and a little chapel.

S 4:00: Reach the hotel at **Mauvoisin (1841m)**.

Stage 3a: Mauvoisin to Cabane FXB Panossière

F From **Mauvoisin**, head W on the road. TL at the next junction. Shortly afterwards, TR and climb on a path. Soon, TR and head W across a grassy plateau. Shortly afterwards, the path turns left and starts to zigzag upwards.

3 0:50: TR at a junction, heading W.

2 1:55: TL at a junction and climb NW across the slope. After a while, the route bends left to head S. At times, the path is steep and exposed: there are chains and steps to assist. Occasionally, the path disappears at sections of rocks: follow waymarks carefully.

1 3:50: Follow red/white waymarks through a rocky moonscape to cross **Col des Otanes (2875m)**. This is the TDC's highest point. Descend SW towards **Glacier de Corbassière**: the views are sublime. At the bottom of the slope, the path bends right and heads N along the lateral moraine of the glacier.

S 4:30: Arrive at **Cabane FXB Panossière (2641m)**.

Col des Otanes (2875m)

4 Cabane de Chanrion/ Rifugio Champillon

This challenging hike through some of the wildest terrain in the Alps involves the crossing of Fenêtre de Durand, a high and remote mountain pass on the frontier between Switzerland and Italy. Travelling between two different countries on foot, across a mountain range, is always an exciting experience but in this case, it is evocative too because Fenêtre de Durand was used during WW2 by refugees fleeing to Switzerland from fascist Italy: in 1943, one of them was Luigi Einaudi who later became the President of Italy. The views on the Swiss side of the pass are magnificent and you can view some of the highest mountains in the Alps: looking N, Pointe d'Otemma (3409m) is the prominent mountain on the fringe of the valley below; behind it, to the left, you will see la Ruinette (3875m) and Mont Blanc de Cheilon (3870m); to its right, you can spot the Dent Blanche (4358m) and the Weisshorn (4505m) on a clear day. On the Italian side of the pass, the vistas are completely different and CW trekkers will witness the peaks of Gran Paradiso National Park for the first time: the highest peak is Gran Paradiso (4061m) itself but it is Grivola (3969m) that dominates your attention.

However, Section 4 is not all about the crossing of Fenêtre de Durand. You will also enjoy a long and very beautiful traverse along the W slopes of Italy's Val d'Ollomont. It is easy to underestimate the time required to hike this undulating part of the route:

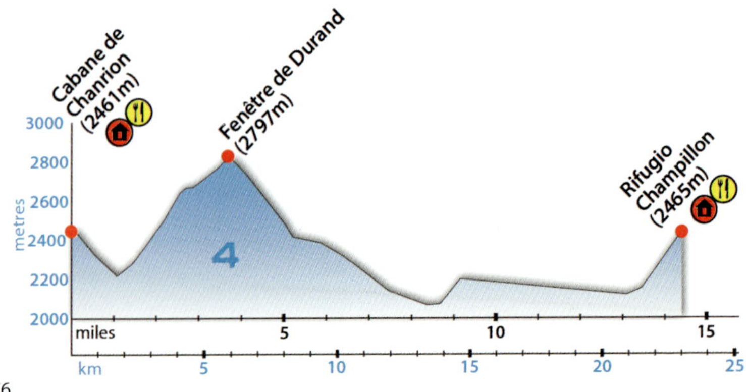

Approaching Fenêtre de Durand

it takes longer than you would think from looking at the maps. Overall, on this stage, you will spend a lot more time in Italy than in Switzerland.

At 23km, Section 4 is the longest and hardest stage of the TDC. Because there is no accommodation mid-section, you must complete it in one go. For this reason, it is best left until later in the trek when you already have a few days' hiking under your belt: this is one of the advantages to starting the trek at BSP/Col du GSB and hiking CW.

Accommodation locations: at each end of the route, there is a wonderfully situated mountain hut: CW trekkers will already have experienced **Cabane de Chanrion** which lies at the N end of Section 4 (see p68). At the S end, you will find **Rifugio Champillon**, the only Italian mountain hut on the TDC. It is a friendly hut with an exquisite location below Mont Chénaille, overlooking Val d'Ollomont. It has lovely food, cold beer and a sauna. If you cannot get a bed at Rifugio Champillon, there is accommodation at **Ollomont** (3.5km OR): hotel, B&Bs and a dormitory.

Trail conditions: generally, paths and tracks are clear and well maintained. On the Italian side of the pass, the paths are sometimes steep, rocky and/or uneven: take care.

Route-finding: the crossing of Fenêtre de Durand involves remote and challenging high mountain terrain. In good conditions, navigation is largely straightforward. However, in poor conditions or low visibility, navigation on certain sections can be tricky. Furthermore, snow can remain near the pass into July, making navigation more difficult. If in doubt, seek the advice of the hut managers at Chanrion/Champillon before setting out.

On the Swiss parts of Section 4, the waymarks are red/white. The Italian parts have yellow arrows and yellow/black diamonds.

		Time	Distance	Ascent CW	Descent CW
Stage 4	Cabane de Chanrion/ Rifugio Champillon	9:00(CW) 9:00(ACW)	23.0km 14.3miles	1203m 3947ft	1199m 3934ft

Accommodation

- Cabane de Chanrion (Stage 3b/4)
- Ollomont (Stage 4; 3.5km OR): hotel; B&Bs; dormitory
- Rifugio Champillon (Stage 4/5a)

Camping

- None

Refreshments/Food

- **Cabane de Chanrion (Stage 3b/4)**
- **Ollomont (Stage 4; 3.5km OR):** restaurants
- **Rifugio Champillon (Stage 4/5a)**

Supplies

- **None**

Escape/Access

- **Ollomont (Stage 4; 3.5km OR):** SVAP (www.svap.it) operates buses to/from Aosta (which is connected to Italy's rail network)

Grand Combin de Grafeneire seen from near Rifugio Champillon

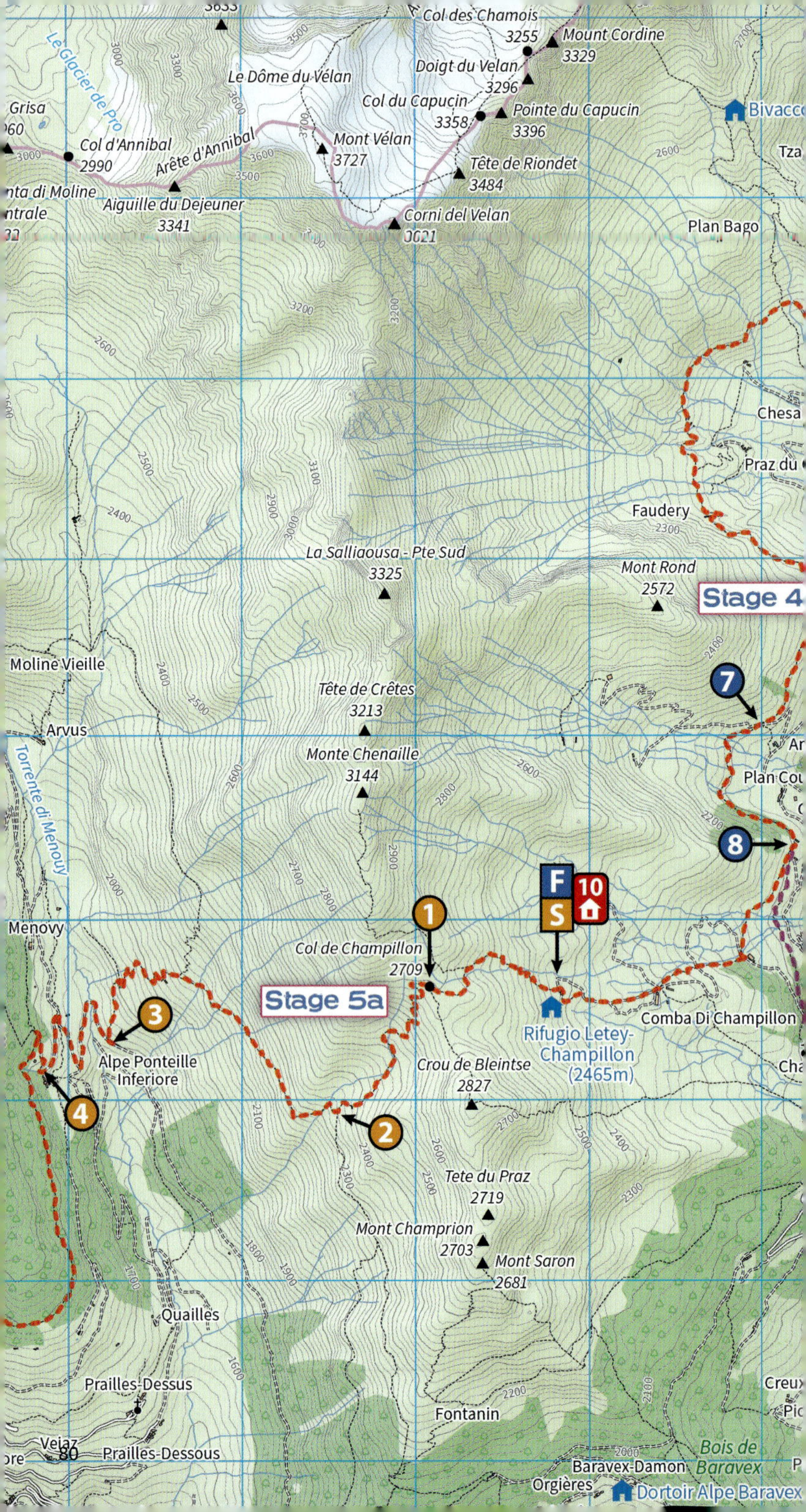

Col des Chamois
3255
Mount Cordine
3329
Doigt du Velan
3296
Le Dôme du Vélan
Col du Capucin
3358
Pointe du Capucin
3396
Bivacco
Le Glacier de Pro
Grisa
Col d'Annibal
2990
Arête d'Annibal
Mont Vélan
3727
Tête de Riondet
3484
Aiguille du Dejeuner
3341
Corni del Velan
Plan Bago
Chesa
Praz du
Faudery
La Salliaousa - Pte Sud
3325
Mont Rond
2572
Stage 4
Moline Vieille
Tête de Crêtes
3213
7
Arvus
Monte Chenaille
3144
Plan Cou
Torrente di Menouy
8
F
10
S
1
Menovy
Col de Champillon
2709
Stage 5a
3
Rifugio Letey-Champillon
(2465m)
Comba Di Champillon
Alpe Ponteille
Inferiore
Crou de Bleintse
2827
4
2
Tete du Praz
2719
Mont Champrion
2703
Mont Saron
2681
Quailles
Prailles-Dessus
Fontanin
Bois de
Baravex
Veiaz
Prailles-Dessous
Baravex-Damon
Orgières
Dortoir Alpe Baravex

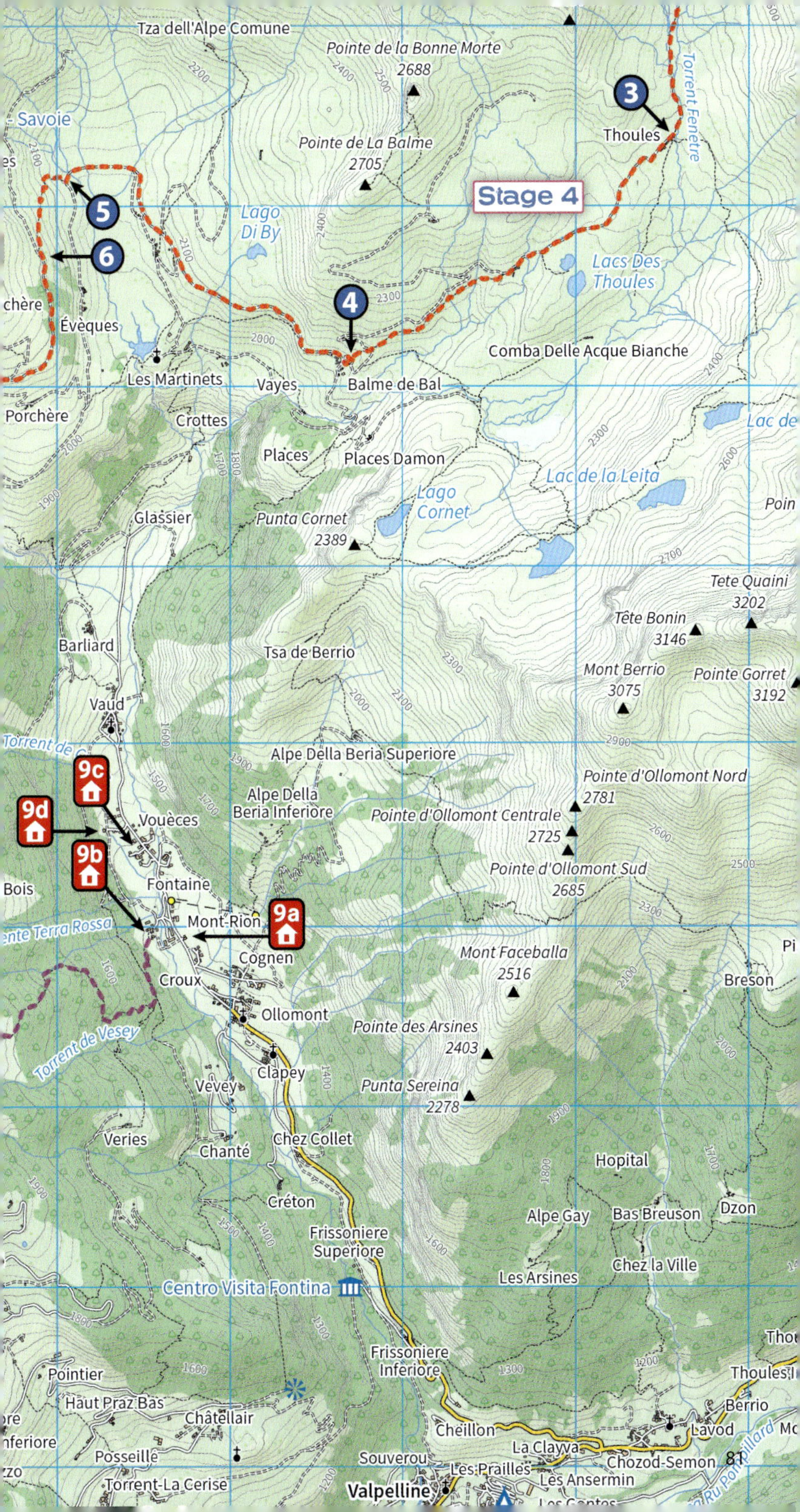

Tza dell'Alpe Comune
Pointe de la Bonne Morte
2688
Savoie
3
Thoules
Torrent Fenetre
Pointe de La Balme
2705
Stage 4
5
Lago
Di By
6
Lacs Des
Thoules
chère
4
Évêques
Comba Delle Acque Bianche
Les Martinets
Vayes
Balme de Bal
Porchère
Crottes
Lac de
Places
Places Damon
Lac de la Leita
Lago
Cornet
Poin
Glassier
Punta Cornet
2389
Tete Quaini
3202
Tête Bonin
3146
Barliard
Tsa de Berrio
Mont Berrio
3075
Pointe Gorret
3192
Vaud
Alpe Della Beria Superiore
Pointe d'Ollomont Nord
2781
9c
Alpe Della
Beria Inferiore
9d
Vouèces
Pointe d'Ollomont Centrale
2725
9b
Pointe d'Ollomont Sud
2685
Bois
Fontaine
9a
Mont-Rion
Cognen
Mont Faceballa
2516
Croux
Breson
Ollomont
Torrent de Vesey
Pointe des Arsines
2403
Clapey
Vevey
Punta Sereina
2278
Veries
Chez Collet
Chanté
Hopital
Créton
Alpe Gay
Bas Breuson
Dzon
Frissoniere
Superiore
Les Arsines
Chez la Ville
Centro Visita Fontina
Frissoniere
Inferiore
Pointier
Thoules
Haut Praz Bas
Châtellair
Berrio
Cheillon
Lavod
La Clayva
Posseille
Souverou
Les Prailles
Chozod-Semon
Les Ansermin
Torrent-La Cerise
Valpelline
Les Gontes

CW (See maps on p73, 80 & 81)

Stage 4: Cabane de Chanrion to Rifugio Champillon

S From **Cabane de Chanrion**, descend S into the valley on a clear path. After a few minutes, keep SH at a junction, still descending. Soon, descend on a track: after a few bends, TR on a narrow path. When you reach a track, TR. A few minutes later, TL on a path and descend towards a stream.

1 0:40: Shortly afterwards, cross a bridge. Then climb in zigzags to the SW. Eventually, the zigzags end but the path continues climbing (now more directly SW).

2 2:40: Keep SH across **Fenêtre de Durand (2797m)**, entering **Italy**. Descend SW into a magnificent grassy valley and head S alongside **Torrent Fenêtre**.

3 4:00: At the farm at **Thoules**, TR onto a track. 20min later, TL down a grassy path. When you meet the track again, keep SH across it.

4 4:50: Shortly afterwards, reach the track again: use it to continue downhill to a junction at some buildings. Head NW, still on the track. Soon, the mountains of **Gran Paradiso National Park** come into view to the S.

5 5:35: TR and climb on a path which is faint and hard to follow. Follow waymarks carefully.

6 6:00: TL along a track. 15-20min later, keep SH at a junction. Just afterwards, TR at another junction, still on a grassy track which contours around the magnificent slopes. Later, take care on narrow/exposed stretches with ropes to assist. At one point, you will also need to squeeze through a gap between rocks.

7 7:30: Keep SH at a junction of tracks, still contouring around the slopes.

8 7:50: TR, crossing a little ridge. Then climb on a grassy path. Cross a track and climb on a steep path into trees. Keep SH uphill past a farm: follow waymarks for the **AV1** long-distance route.

F 9:00: Arrive at **Rifugio Champillon (2465m)**.

ACW (See maps on p81, 80 & 73)

Stage 4: Rifugio Champillon to Cabane de Chanrion

F From **Rifugio Champillon**, descend E, following waymarks for the **AV1** long-distance route. Keep SH downhill past a farm. Descend through trees to reach a junction: TL, leaving the **AV1**. Just afterwards, keep SH across a track and descend N on a grassy path.

8 0:40: TL at a junction. The route contours around the slopes.

7 1:00: Keep SH at a junction of tracks and continue to contour around the slopes. Later, take care on narrow/exposed stretches with ropes to assist. At one point, you will also need to squeeze through a gap between rocks. Ignore any paths to the left/right which climb/descend more steeply.

6 2:30: TR onto a path (easy to miss). It is faint: follow waymarks carefully.

5 2:45: TL along a track. You should see the mountains of **Gran Paradiso National Park** to the S: the summit of **Gran Paradiso (4061m)** is visible but **Grivola (3969m)** is the peak that dominates. After a while, TL at a junction at some buildings and climb on the track.

4 3:45: Shortly afterwards, climb E on a path, leaving the track. Soon, meet the track again: keep SH across it and continue climbing on the path. Later, when you meet the track once again, keep SH and head NE along it.

3 5:00: At the farm at **Thoules**, TL onto a path which climbs N alongside **Torrent Fenêtre**. Follow the path when it crosses the stream and climb NE.

2 6:45: Keep SH across **Fenêtre de Durand (2797m)**, entering **Switzerland**. Descend NE.

1 8:00: Cross a bridge over a stream. Then TR and climb on a path. Shortly afterwards, TR and head S on a track. A few minutes later, TL and climb on a path. When you reach a track, TL and climb. After a few bends, TL and climb N on a path.

S 9:00: Arrive at **Cabane de Chanrion (2461m)**.

Cabane de Chanrion (Stage 3b/4)

5 Rifugio Champillon/ Col du Grand-St-Bernard

The scenery on Section 5 is fabulous. Stage 5a displays more of the wild and beautiful terrain that CW trekkers will have witnessed on previous stages. The crossing of Col de Champillon comes early in the day so you could experience its wonderful views at sunrise if you were prepared to skip breakfast. Afterwards, the descent into the tranquil Vallon de Menouve is even more beautiful, with Mont Blanc appearing to the W. Continuing W, the path enters woodland as it travels towards the lovely village of St-Rhémy in the Grand-St-Bernard valley. From St-Rhémy, Stage 5b leads CW trekkers up the E side of the GSB valley to Col du GSB (see p89). A winding road also climbs the valley on its way to the col (where it enters Switzerland): although it would be an exaggeration to state that the road enhances the scenery, it is fair to say that the sight of its twists and turns, as it works its way upwards, are aesthetically very pleasing and this is still a very beautiful landscape.

For ACW trekkers, the day starts with a long descent from Col de GSB to St-Rhémy (Stage 5b). The departure from St-Rhémy along Stage 5a marks the start of many days of hiking through remote terrain: other than the tiny Mauvoisin (Stage 3a/3b), no villages are entered until you reach BSP.

In either direction, Section 5 is challenging unless you split it by spending the night at St-Rhémy. The total distance is more than 22km and there is more than 1300m of ascent and descent.

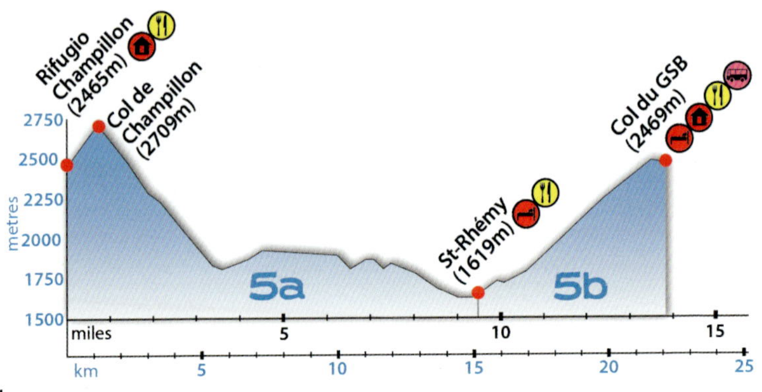

The approach to Col du GSB

Accommodation locations: a stay at **Col du GSB** is a highlight of the TDC. On the Swiss side of the pass, you can stay and eat at the historic **Hospice** (monastery; see p93) which traditionally provided accommodation to pilgrims heading towards Rome on the Via Francigena (see p92): this part of the monastery is on the S side of the road and it also houses the chapel and a glittering treasury (which is stuffed full of relics). It has private rooms and dormitory beds. There is also a more modern hotel, **Auberge de l'Hospice**, which has a good restaurant/bar: it is located within the monastery complex, in the building on the N side of the road which also houses the museum, kennels for the St Bernard dogs (see p93) and a souvenir shop. There are also a couple of restaurants, a hotel and souvenir shops on the Italian side of the pass.

If you feel like stopping mid-section, there is a lovely hotel at **St-Rhémy**. Alternatively, **St-Rhémy-en-Bosses** (2km OR from St-Rhémy) has a hotel and some B&Bs. ACW trekkers can stay at the excellent **Rifugio Champillon**: see p77.

Trail conditions: on Stage 5a, the path between (2) and (3) is steep and occasionally exposed. On Stage 5b, the path is faint between (1) and (2). Otherwise, Section 5's paths/tracks are largely clear, well maintained and straightforward to negotiate.

Route-finding: Section 5a involves crossing remote and challenging high mountain terrain. In good conditions, navigation is largely straightforward. However, in poor conditions or low visibility, navigation on certain sections can be tricky. Between (3) and St-Rhémy, the route enters forest where there is a confusing labyrinth of different paths/tracks: follow signs/waymarks carefully.

		Time	Distance	Ascent CW	Descent CW
Stage 5a	Rifugio Champillon/ St-Rhémy	4:45(CW) 6:15(ACW)	15.1km 9.4miles	450m 1476ft	1296m 4252ft
Stage 5b	St-Rhémy/ Col du GSB	3:15(CW) 2:15(ACW)	7.0km 4.4miles	892m 2927ft	42m 138ft

Accommodation

- **Rifugio Champillon (Stage 4/5a)**
- **St-Rhémy (Stage 5a/5b):** Suisse Locanda di Borgo
- **St-Rhémy-en-Bosses (Stage 5a/5b; 2km OR):** hotel; B&Bs
- **Col du GSB (Stage 5b/6/v6):** Hospice; Auberge de l'Hospice; Hotel Italia

Camping

- **None**

Refreshments/Food

- **Rifugio Champillon (Stage 4/5a)**
- **St-Rhémy (Stage 5a/5b):** Suisse Locanda di Borgo
- **St-Rhémy-en-Bosses (Stage 5a/5b; 2km OR):** restaurant
- **1**: restaurant/bar
- **Col du GSB (Stage 5b/6/v6):** restaurants; cafés

Supplies

- **St-Rhémy (Stage 5a/5b):** Prosciuttificio de Bosses (at the bottom of the village) sells fabulous locally made hams, salamis and other cured meats
- **St-Rhémy-en-Bosses (Stage 5a/5b; 2km OR):** small grocery store

Escape/Access

- **St-Rhémy-en-Bosses (Stage 5a/5b; 2km OR):** Arriva (www.aosta.arriva.it) operates buses to/from Aosta. From Aosta, you can travel by train throughout Italy. Furthermore, TMR operates bus 12.211 between Aosta and Martigny (via BSP and Orsières)
- **Col du GSB (Stage 5b/6/v6):** bus 210 to BSP and Orsières

The Italian side of Col du GSB

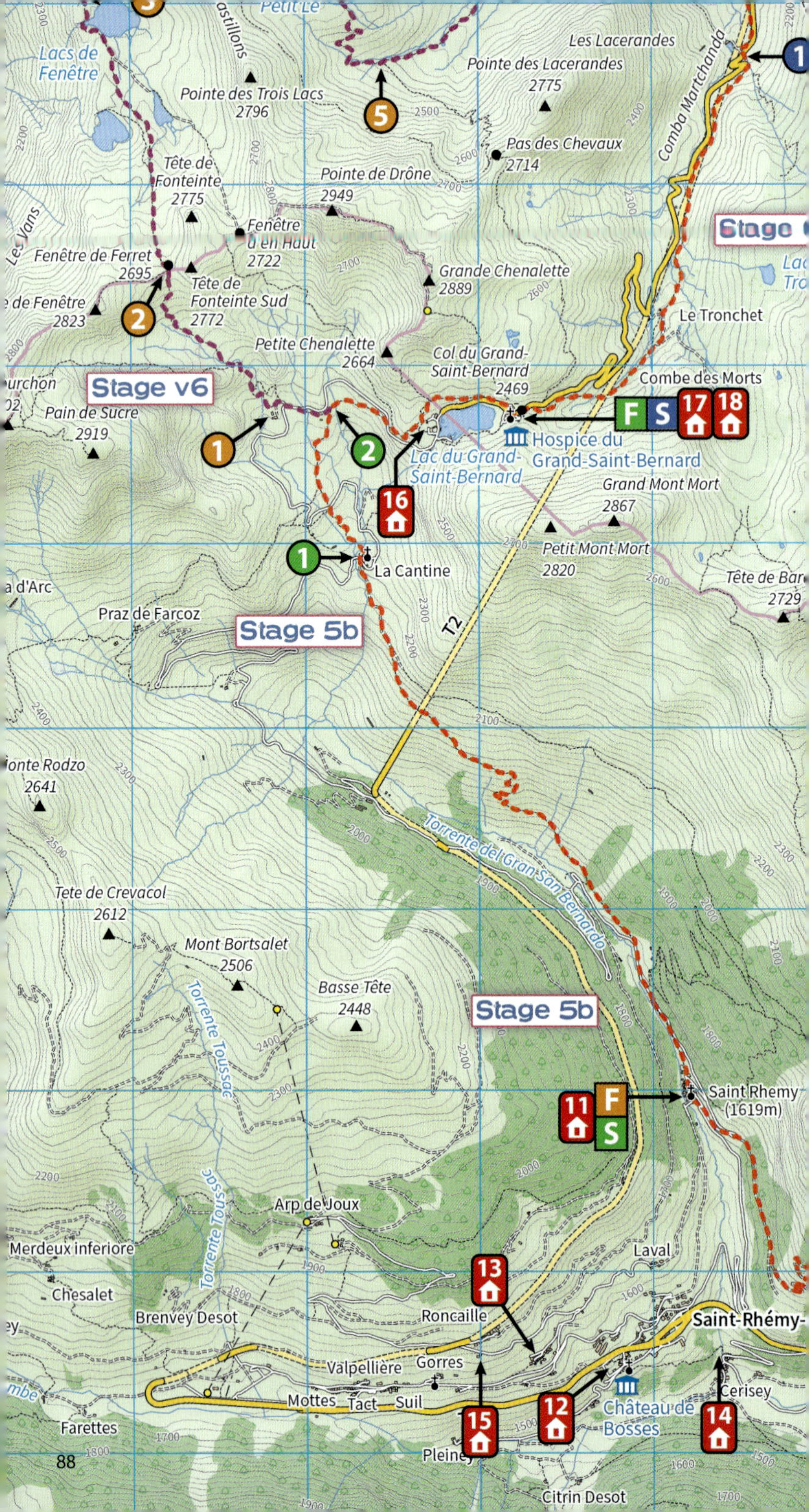
Lacs de Fenêtre
Pointe des Trois Lacs 2796
Les Lacerandes
Pointe des Lacerandes 2775
Pas des Chevaux 2714
Comba Marchanda
Tête de Fonteinte 2775
Pointe de Drône 2949
Fenêtre d'en Haut 2722
Fenêtre de Ferret 2695
Tête de Fonteinte Sud 2772
Grande Chenalette 2889
Le Tronchet
Petite Chenalette 2664
Col du Grand-Saint-Bernard 2469
Combe des Morts
Stage v6
Pain de Sucre 2919
Lac du Grand-Saint-Bernard
Hospice du Grand-Saint-Bernard
Grand Mont Mort 2867
Petit Mont Mort 2820
La Cantine
Tête de Bar 2729
Praz de Farcoz
Stage 5b
T2
Torrente del Gran San Bernardo
Tete de Crevacol 2612
Mont Bortsalet 2506
Basse Tête 2448
Torrente Toussac
Saint Rhemy (1619m)
Arp de Joux
Merdeux inferiore
Laval
Chesalet
Brenvey Desot
Roncaille
Saint-Rhémy-
Valpellière
Gorres
Cerisey
Mottes
Tact
Suil
Château de Bosses
Farettes
Pleiney
Citrin Desot

Grand-St-Bernard Pass

At 2469m, the Col du GSB is Switzerland's third highest road pass. It links Martigny with Aosta in Italy. It sits on the watershed of the Rhône valley (to the N) and the Po valley (to the S). It was named after St-Bernard who was canonized in the 16th Century. It has been used by travellers since the Bronze Age. The Romans completed a road over the pass around 43CE and, near the top, constructed an official building and a temple to Jupiter. Today, a cross (dating from 1816) marks the site of the temple which was located on a knoll on the Italian side of the pass. The statue of St-Bernard (erected in 1905) marks the site of the other building. There are many Roman artefacts in the monastery museum.

Napoleon Bonaparte crossed the pass in 1800 with an army of 40,000, on the way to attack the Austrian army which had laid siege to French-occupied Genoa. Although the Austrian army had much greater numbers, the wily Napoleon defeated them at the battles of Montebello and Marengo. The five famous portraits, painted in 1801-05, by Jacques-Louis David show Napoleon crossing the pass on a stallion but, in fact, he crossed on the back of a mule which plays a part in a heart-warming sub-plot. The story goes that, on the climb to the pass, Napoleon spent time discussing affairs of the heart with a young mule driver, Pierre Nicholas Dorsaz, who was unaware of the identity of his famous companion. At the top, Napoleon offered him a reward and Dorsaz asked for the mule. Napoleon gave him the mule and a note for the army quartermaster. It was only when Dorsaz submitted the note that he found out that his companion had been Napoleon who had awarded him a house and farmland to enable him to marry his sweetheart.

The pass can only be crossed by vehicles between June and September. In 1964, the GSB tunnel opened, allowing cars to bypass the col by driving straight through the mountain. The Tour de France, the world's most famous cycling race, has visited the pass five times.

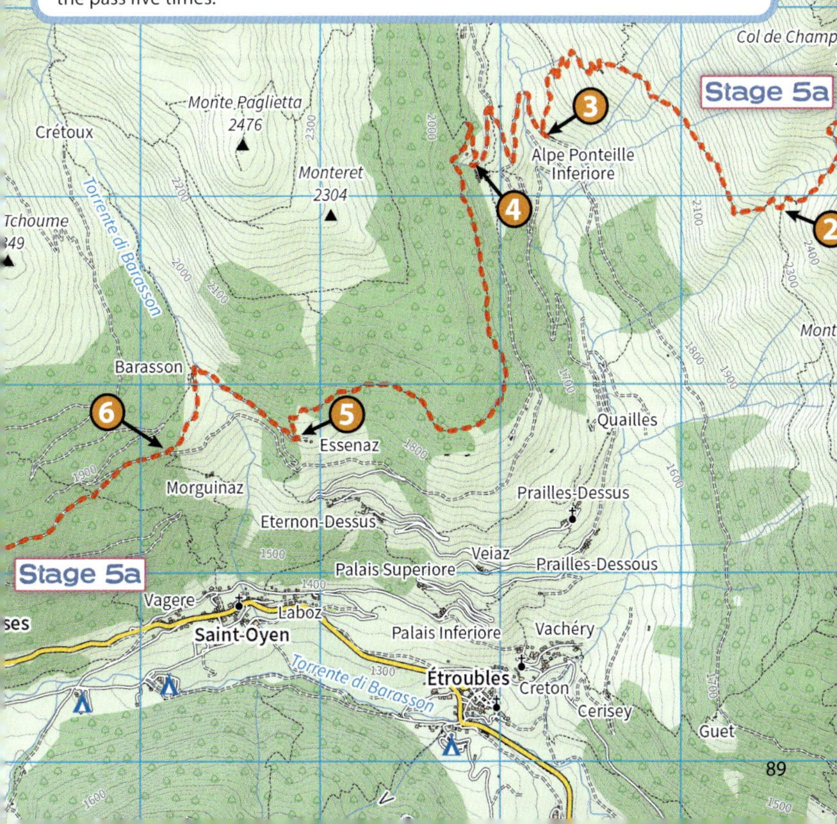

CW (See maps on p80, 89 & 88)

Stage 5a: Rifugio Champillon to St-Rhémy

S From **Rifugio Champillon**, climb steeply W.

1 0:45: Cross **Col de Champillon (2709m)**. Then descend a series of zigzags to the SW: soon there are superb views of Mont Blanc to the W.

2 1:20: TR at a junction, now heading W but remaining on the main path. Soon the path bends right (as it crosses a spur) and descends NW across the slope. After a while, zigzag down the slope to the W.

3 2:15: Near the valley floor, at the buildings of **Alpe Ponteille Inferiore**, TR onto a track. The track soon bends left, crosses a stream and climbs S. After a few minutes, TR at a junction, still climbing on a track. 5min later, TL at a junction.

4 2:45: TR and climb steeply on a path. Soon the gradient levels as you head S.

5 3:45: After descending for a while, TR on a track and climb gently. 10min later, TL and head S past a farm: continue on a grassy path, contouring around the slopes.

6 4:00: TR on a track, joining the **AV1** long-distance trail (follow AV1 waymarks until St-Rhémy). Shortly afterwards, TL at a fork, descending on a track. TL onto a road and descend.

F 4:45: 5min later, reach the village of **St-Rhémy (1619m)**.

Stage 5b: St-Rhémy to Col du GSB

S Head uphill through **St-Rhémy**. At the top of the village, keep SH, climbing on a grassy path. TL up the road. Shortly afterwards, ignore a path (no.13) on the right. Take the next path on the right (no.13B) which climbs NW.

1 2:10: Keep SH across the road and continue climbing on a path. 10min later, cross the road again and climb N on a path.

2 2:45: TR at a junction and soon climb on the old cobbled pilgrims' path. Keep SH across the road: take great care as vehicles travel fast round the blind corner. Then climb a path through rock to a **statue of St-Bernard** near the restaurants on the Italian side of Col du GSB. Follow waymarks N up through rocks to cross the **Italy/Switzerland border**. The route then heads E just above the road (again following the old pilgrims' path to the col).

F 3:15: 5min later, reach the **monastery** at **Col du GSB (2469m)**.

Alternative routes between the St-Bernard statue and F

An alternative path runs along the S shore of Lac du GSB: it is lovely but more uneven underfoot. Or, if you are tired, you could simply walk along the road.

ACW (See maps on p88, 89 & 80)

Stage 5b: Col du GSB to St-Rhémy

F From the **monastery** at **Col du GSB**, head W on the path above the road and lake. Above the NW corner of the lake, cross the **Italy/Switzerland border**. Then descend S through rocks to a **statue of St-Bernard**. Now follow a path W through rocks to reach the road: take care crossing it (blind corner). Descend initially NW on the old cobbled pilgrims' path.

2 0:25: TL at a junction and descend S through pastures. When you reach the road, keep SH across it.

1 0:45: Keep SH across the road again and continue descending on a path. Soon, TR at a fork (path 13B). Eventually, when you reach the road again, keep SH down it. A few minutes later, TR on a path.

S 2:15: Shortly afterwards, reach the village of **St-Rhémy (1619m)**.

Stage 5a: St-Rhémy to Rifugio Champillon

F From the bottom of **St-Rhémy**, head SE up the road. When you reach a hairpin bend, keep SH on a track (which soon climbs): follow waymarks for the **AV1** long-distance trail.

6 1:00: TL and climb on a path, leaving the AV1. TR after a farm and head SE on a track.

5 1:15: 10min later, TL at a junction.

4 2:20: TL and head N on a track. TR at the next junction. TL at the following junction. After a few minutes, the track bends right, crosses a stream and heads S.

3 2:45: At the buildings of **Alpe Ponteille Inferiore**, TL and climb on a path. Soon zigzag upwards to the E. Then contour SE across the slopes. The path bends left as it crosses a spur.

2 4:30: 5min later, TL at a junction and climb. Soon the path zigzags up to the N.

1 5:50: Cross **Col de Champillon (2709m)**. Then descend E.

S 6:15: Arrive at **Rifugio Champillon (2465m)**.

Mont Blanc viewed from the W side of Col de Champillon (Stage 5a)

Via Francigena

Via Francigena means 'road that originates in France'. It is an ancient trade road and pilgrimage route that runs from the English city of Canterbury through France and Switzerland to Rome: from there, it continues to Puglia in southern Italy. It was an important pilgrimage route in the Middle Ages for travellers seeking to visit Rome. In fact, it was not an organised single route like a Roman road. There were several possible itineraries which changed over the centuries but generally, the route passed from cathedral to cathedral. In recent decades, with the increase in popularity of long-distance trekking, interest in the Via Francigena has been revived. The Col du GSB is where it crosses the Alpine chain. The TDC follows the route of the Via Francigena between BSP and St-Rhémy (Stages 5b and 6).

The monastery at the Swiss side of Col du GSB

Grand-St-Bernard Monastery & St-Bernard Dogs

The Grand-St-Bernard Monastery (or Hospice) is situated at 2469m on the Swiss side of an Alpine pass now known as the Col du Grand-St-Bernard (see p89). It was founded in 1050 by St. Bernard of Mont-Joux, the Archdeacon of Aosta, to provide shelter to travellers crossing the pass (which was then an important gateway between northern and southern Europe). It has operated without interruption ever since, a period of almost 1000 years.

Initially, the role of the Hospice was to provide refuge from bandits who plagued the pass. But soon it was also assisting in the rescue of travellers lost or trapped in snow near the pass. At some point in the 17th century, the monks started using dogs to assist in rescues. They bred large dogs specifically to negotiate deep snow and with a keen sense of smell so that they could locate people lost in it. This breed became known as St-Bernard after the founder of the Hospice. It is said that the St-Bernards required little training, with young dogs learning their trade by watching the older ones.

Technological advances and the construction of the modern road and tunnel have made the dogs obsolete for the purposes of rescues: the last recorded use of a St-Bernard in an Alpine rescue was in 1955. Nevertheless, the Hospice continued to breed them until 2004 when they sold the last 18 dogs to the Barry Foundation. Today, the foundation has around 35 dogs including the ones that you can see in the kennels at the Hospice. Sadly, it is a myth that the St-Bernards carried a cask of brandy around their necks.

6 Col du Grand-St-Bernard/ Bourg-St-Pierre

Unless intending to walk the Stage v6 variant, CW trekkers who started the trek in BSP have, by now, completed most of the hard work: all that remains is a straightforward descent (along the floor of the Val d'Entremont) to return to BSP. The landscape is beautiful with grassy, flower-filled pastures surrounded by high peaks, however, this relatively short stage has none of the far-reaching panoramas that you will have enjoyed on previous stages: accordingly, if you are travelling CW, you have the time and energy, and the weather is fine, we highly recommend that you choose Stage v6 instead (see p102).

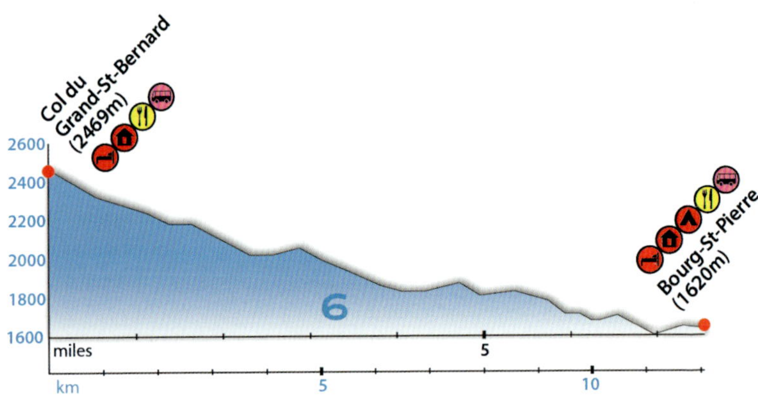

Mont Vélan towers over Val d'Entremont

For ACW trekkers, Section 6 is much harder, especially for those who start the trek at BSP and will therefore have a long climb on the first day. That said, although the elevation gain is more than 1000m, the terrain is not particularly difficult and it is a reasonably good stage for getting your head and legs into the game. The valley scenery is perfect for a first day too, leaving the very best landscapes for later on in the trek.

Accommodation locations: CW trekkers can stay at **BSP** (see p49) and ACW trekkers stay at **Col du GSB** (see p85). There is no accommodation mid-stage.

Trail conditions: paths and tracks are clear, well-maintained and straightforward to negotiate.

Route-finding: straightforward. Most significant junctions have signposts and waymarks (yellow/black diamonds).

		Time	Distance	Ascent CW	Descent CW
Stage 6	Col du GSB/ Bourg-St-Pierre	3:40(CW) 5:20(ACW)	12.1km 7.5miles	206m 676ft	1055m 3461ft

Accommodation

- **Col du GSB (Stage 5b/6/v6):** Hospice; Auberge de l'Hospice; Hotel Italia
- **BSP (Stage 1/6/v6):** hotels; dormitory beds at Hotel du Crêt

Camping

- **BSP (Stage 1/6/v6):** Camping Grand Saint Bernard

The TDC descends into the Val d'Entremont

Refreshments/Food

- **Col du Grand-St-Bernard (Stage 5b/6/v6):** restaurants; cafés
- **Café at the N end of Lac des Toules**
- **BSP (Stage 1/6/v6):** restaurants

Supplies

- **BSP (Stage 1/6/v6):** small shop beside service station (snacks/drinks)

Escape/Access

- **Col du GSB (Stage 5b/6/v6):** bus 210 to/from BSP and Orsières
- **BSP (Stage 1/6/v6):** bus 210 to/from Orsières and Col du GSB; TMR bus 12.211 to Aosta through the GSB Tunnel (avoiding Col du GSB)

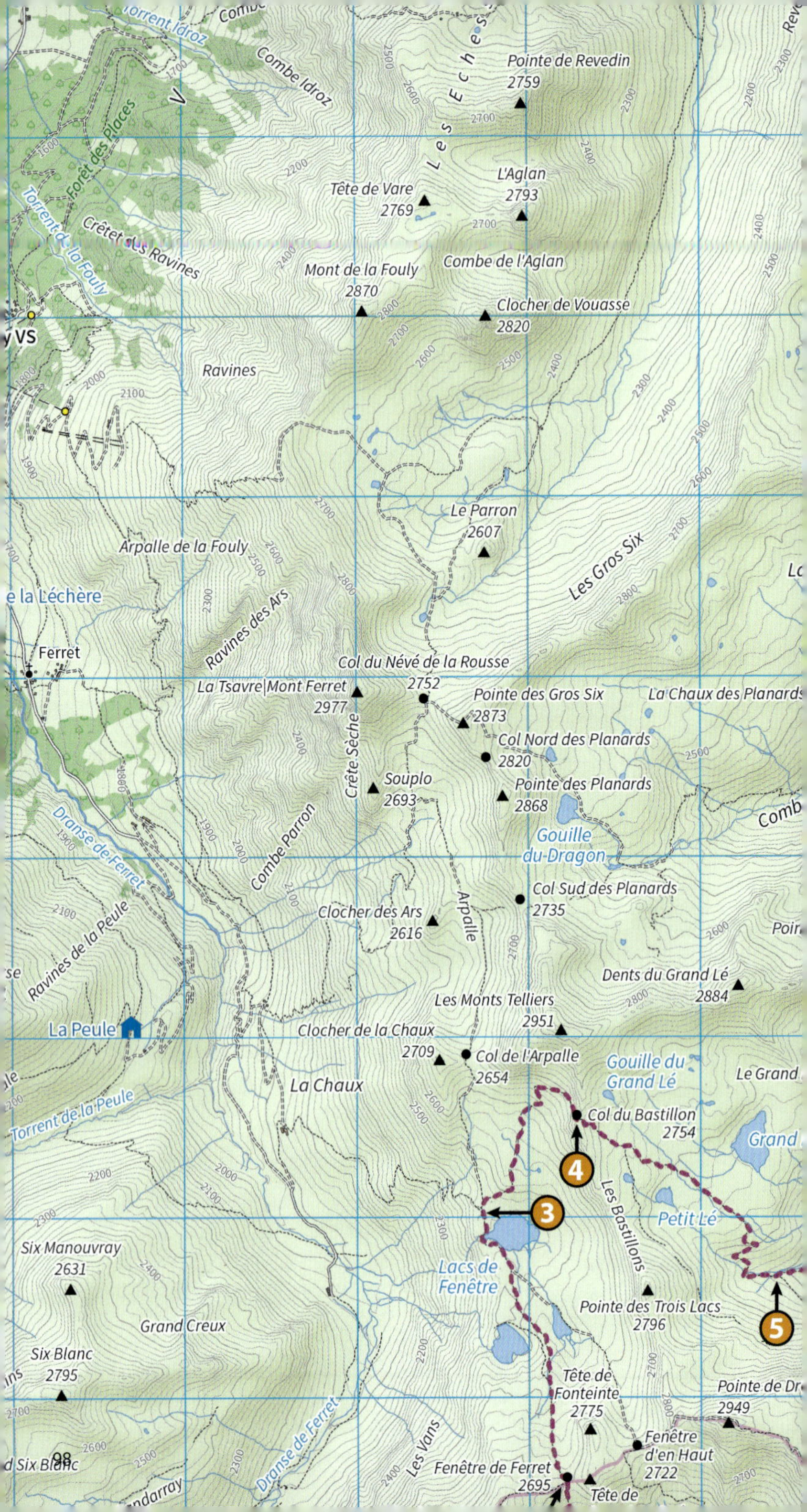

Torrent Idroz
Combe Idroz
Pointe de Revedin
2759
Les Eches
Forêt des Places
Tête de Vare
2769
L'Aglan
2793
Torrent de la Fouly
Crêtet des Ravines
Combe de l'Aglan
Mont de la Fouly
2870
Clocher de Vouasse
2820
Ravines
Le Parron
2607
Les Gros Six
Arpalle de la Fouly
Ravines des Ars
Ferret
Col du Névé de la Rousse
2752
La Tsavre|Mont Ferret
2977
Pointe des Gros Six
2873
La Chaux des Planards
Col Nord des Planards
2820
Crête Sèche
Souplo
2693
Pointe des Planards
2868
Gouille du Dragon
Dranse de Ferret
Combe Parron
Col Sud des Planards
2735
Clocher des Ars
2616
Arpalle
Ravines de la Peule
Dents du Grand Lé
2884
Les Monts Telliers
2951
La Peule
Clocher de la Chaux
2709
Col de l'Arpalle
2654
Gouille du Grand Lé
Le Grand
La Chaux
Torrent de la Peule
Col du Bastillon
2754
4
3
Les Bastillons
Petit Lé
Six Manouvray
2631
Lacs de Fenêtre
Pointe des Trois Lacs
2796
5
Grand Creux
Six Blanc
2795
Tête de Fonteinte
2775
Pointe de Dr
2949
Fenêtre d'en Haut
2722
Dranse de Ferret
Les Vans
Fenêtre de Ferret
2695
Tête de

Bourg-St-Pierre
(1620m)
Jardin Alpin La Linnaea
Stage 6
Lac des Toules
La Chaux de la Lette
Le Mourin
2765
Le Pey
2590
La Chaux de Tsousse
Bonhomme de Ts
2729
Croix de Tsousse
2829
Torrent des Erbets
Torrent de Pieudet
Pointe des Plans Sades
2673
La Chaux du Plan du Jeu
Mont de Pro
2803
Les Plans Sades
Cabane du Plan du Jeu
Les Darreys
Pointe de Godegotte
2749
Stage v6
Les Fouéreuses
Punta di Moline Ovest
3020
Col de Moline
2906
Punta di Crête Sèche
2951
Les Lacerandes
Pointe des Lacerandes
2775
Comba Martchanda
Les Places
Becs Noirs
Menouve
Monte di Menouve
3051
Pas des Chevaux
2714
Bec Noir
2797
Col Nord de Menouve
2772
Col Sud de Menouve
2755
Lac des Tronchets
Tête Rouge
L'Eudenna
Le Creux de Mourin
Torrent du Va

CW (See maps on p88 & 99)

Stage 6: Col du GSB to Bourg-St-Pierre

S From the **monastery**, head E along the road. Shortly afterwards, TR and descend steeply on a path. 20min later, just after crossing a stream, TR at a fork to reach a grassy track: TL to head N, still descending. 5min later, cross a bridge over a stream.

1 0:45: Cross the road and keep SH on a track. Shortly afterwards, TR at a junction, back towards the road. Shortly after that, TL and descend on a path. 10min later, TL down a track.

2 1:10: Just after a hairpin bend, TR and climb steeply on a path. There are plenty of marmots here. Shortly afterwards, go through a gate and TR: head NE on a path. Keep SH at any junctions. The path soon bends left to head N along the slopes above **Lac des Toules**.

3 2:35: Shortly after crossing a bridge, reach a track: take the right fork. At the N end of the lake, pass a café. 5min later, just after a right-hand bend in the track, TL down a steep path (no waymarks; easy to miss). 5min later, TL onto another path: head N along **Val d'Entremont**.

4 3:25: TR at a junction. TL onto a road.

F 3:40: Shortly afterwards, enter **Bourg-St-Pierre (1620m)**.

ACW (See maps on p99 & 88)

Stage 6: Bourg-St-Pierre to Col du GSB

F Head S on **Rue du Bourg** through the centre of **BSP**. Shortly after exiting the village, TR on a path which soon heads S below the road.

4 0:15: TL and head S on a track along **Val d'Entremont**. Keep SH when the track narrows to a path. 5min later, TR at a fork and climb more steeply. Soon, TR onto a track, continuing upwards. 5min later, keep SH at a junction and pass a café at the N end of **Lac des Toules**. Head S on a track, along the slopes above the lake.

3 1:45: At a hairpin bend, keep SH on a path. Shortly afterwards, cross a bridge. After the lake, the path bends gradually right: keep SH at any junctions.

2 3:30: At **la Pierre**, you have two options. For **Stage 6**, TL and go through a gate: alternatively, for **Stage v6**, climb SW. Follow a path heading E, downhill. Shortly afterwards, TL onto a track and follow it downhill. There are plenty of marmots here. Shortly after the track bends left, TR onto a path and climb parallel to the road. Soon, TR onto a track. Just afterwards TL at a junction.

1 4:00: Just afterwards, keep SH across the road and climb on a path. 5min after a bridge over a stream, reach a grassy track: head S. Soon, at a hairpin bend, keep SH on a path, leaving the track. Now climb SW. Later, TL onto the road.

S 5:20: Shortly afterwards, reach the **monastery** at **Col du GSB (2469m)**.

The village of Orsières (Stage v1)

v6 Col du Grand-St-Bernard/ Bourg-St-Pierre (high route via Fenêtre de Ferret)

This incredible stage is not an official TDC variant. We have designed it specifically to offer trekkers a more exciting high-altitude alternative to the official Stage 6 route (which is a lower-level valley hike). It enables CW trekkers to finish the TDC on a high and, on a fine day, it is unquestionably a highlight of the trek. Only one ridge separates the Mont Blanc Massif from Col du GSB. Furthermore, that ridge is only a short climb from the col and the vistas from the top of the ridge are sublime (offering the best views of the Mont Blanc Massif on the entire trek). In our opinion, therefore, it seems crazy not to try to incorporate this route into your itinerary if the weather is favourable.

Our route uses one magnificent pass to cross to the W side of the ridge and then another pass to return to the E side again. For CW trekkers, the first col is Fenêtre de Ferret: it is a fabulous place but the finest views are still ahead. Descending N, you will find a group of exquisite lakes (known as Lacs de Fenêtre) which have the Mont Blanc Massif as a backdrop: it is jaw-droppingly beautiful. And there is more to come because as you climb towards the second col, Col du Bastillon, the views get even better. From the top, the 360° panorama is extraordinary: in fact, this is probably the

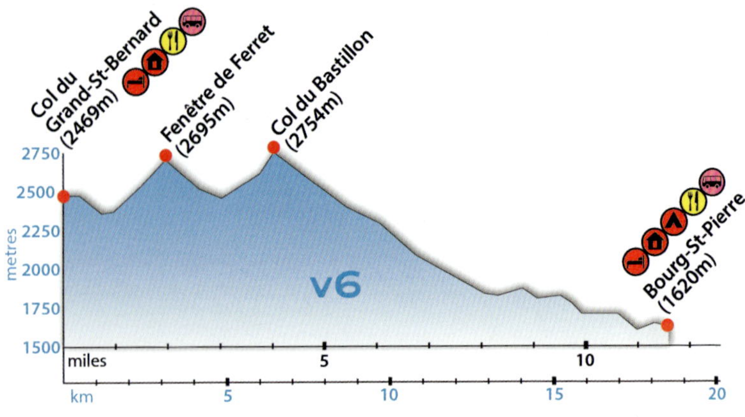

Col du Bastillon

most comprehensive viewpoint on the entire trek. To the W, the Mont Blanc Massif is laid out in full splendour and the Grandes Jorasses and Mont Dolent look incredible from this angle; to the E, you can see Mont Vélan and the Combins Massif; to the S, the summits of Gran Paradiso National Park are visible. It is simply unforgettable. Afterwards, you pass more spectacular lakes as you drop though the pastures to the E to rejoin the main TDC route again at la Pierre.

Although long, Section v6 is fairly manageable for CW trekkers who have much less altitude gain to endure because they start at a higher altitude (2469m). ACW trekkers, on the other hand, start Stage v6 from BSP which sits at 1620m: this means that they face more than 1600m of climbing (which will be too much for some, especially on the first day of the trek).

Accommodation locations: CW trekkers can stay at **BSP** (see p49) and ACW trekkers stay at **Col du GSB** (see p85). There is no accommodation mid-stage.

Trail conditions: this route involves remote and challenging high mountain terrain. Generally, paths and tracks are clear, well-maintained and straightforward to negotiate. However, some sections are steep and rocky: in particular, the paths on the S side of Fenêtre de Ferret and both sides of Col du Bastillon are sometimes steep and a little unstable. The path on the W side of Col du Bastillon is also very exposed: take care as a fall could be serious.

Route-finding: straightforward in good conditions. Most significant junctions have signposts/waymarks. Sometimes, snow can remain on the highest sections of the route into July, making navigation more difficult. Do not attempt this route in bad weather or low visibility.

		Time	Distance	Ascent CW	Descent CW
Stage v6	Col du GSB/ Bourg-St-Pierre	6:45(CW) 8:00(ACW)	18.5km 11.5miles	815m 2674ft	1664m 5460ft

Accommodation

- **Col du GSB (Stage 5b/6/v6):** Hospice; Auberge de l'Hospice; Hotel Italia
- **BSP (Stage 1/6/v6):** hotels; dormitory beds at Hotel du Crêt

Camping

- **BSP (Stage 1/6/v6):** Camping Grand Saint Bernard

One of the spectacular Lacs de Fenêtre

Refreshments/Food

- **Col du Grand-St-Bernard (Stage 5b/6/v6):** restaurants; cafés
- **1**: Alpeggio lo Baou (farm shop and café)
- **Café at the N end of Lac des Toules**
- **BSP (Stage 1/6/v6):** restaurants

Supplies

- **BSP (Stage 1/6/v6):** small shop beside service station (snacks/drinks)

Escape/Access

- **Col du GSB (Stage 5b/6/v6):** bus 210 to/from BSP and Orsières
- **BSP (Stage 1/6/v6):** bus 210 to/from Orsières and Col du GSB; TMR bus 12.211 to Aosta through the GSB Tunnel (avoiding Col du GSB)

CW (See maps on p88, 98 & 99)

Stage v6: Col du GSB to Bourg-St-Pierre

S From the **monastery** at **Col du GSB**, head W on the path above the road and lake. Above the NW corner of the lake, cross the **Italy/Switzerland border**. Then descend S through rocks to the **statue of St-Bernard**. Now follow a path W through rocks to reach the road: take care crossing it (blind corner). Descend initially NW on the old cobbled pilgrims' path.

2 0:25: Keep SH at the junction passed on Stage 5b, heading W on path 13A.

1 0:30: Cross the road and enter a parking area beside **Alpeggio lo Baou** (farm shop and café). Pick up path 13A which heads steeply uphill (yellow arrows). 20min later, TR at a fork, staying on path 13A: afterwards, the waymarks are red/white.

2 1:15: Keep SH across **Fenêtre de Ferret (2695m)**, entering **Switzerland** again ('Lacs de Fenêtre'). The path descends N and passes between the first two lakes (**Lacs de Fenêtre**). The **Mont Blanc Massif** is visible to the W. From the left side of the largest lake, continue N.

3 1:50: TR at a junction and climb ('Col du Bastillon'). Shortly afterwards, TR at a fork, staying on the main path which will climb NE (red/white waymarks and posts). Later, a narrow path heads along the sheer edge of a slope: take care as the drops are steep.

4 3:00: Cross **Col du Bastillon (2754m)** and descend SE on a steep, loose path. Pass some more magnificent lakes.

5 3:35: At a junction (rock with signs on it), TL and descend along the valley floor.

6 4:05: TL at a junction (easy to miss) and cross the stream. Then continue downhill alongside the stream.

2 4:20: At **la Pierre**, reach a junction beside a gate. This is where **Stage v6** and **Stage 6** converge. TL and head NE on a path. Keep SH at any junctions. The path soon bends left to head N along the slopes above **Lac des Toules**.

3 5:40: Shortly after crossing a bridge, reach a track: take the right fork. At the N end of the lake, pass a café. 5min later, just after a right-hand bend in the track, TL down a steep path (no waymarks; easy to miss). 5min later, TL onto another path: head N along **Val d'Entremont**.

4 6:30: TR at a junction. TL onto a road.

F 6:45: Shortly afterwards, enter **BSP (1620m)**.

Descending towards Val d'Entremont

ACW (See maps on p99, 98 & 88)

Stage v6: Bourg-St-Pierre to Col du GSB

F Head S on **Rue du Bourg** through the centre of **BSP**. Shortly after exiting the village, TR on a path which soon heads S below the road.

4 0:15: TL and head S on a track along **Val d'Entremont**. Keep SH when the track narrows to a path. 5min later, TR at a fork and climb more steeply. Soon, TR onto a track, continuing upwards. 5min later, keep SH at a junction and pass a café at the N end of **Lac des Toules**. Head S on a track, along the slopes above the lake.

3 1:45: At a hairpin bend, keep SH on a path. Shortly afterwards, cross a bridge. After the lake, the path bends gradually right: keep SH at any junctions.

2 3:30: At **la Pierre**, reach a junction beside a gate. For **Stage v6**, TR and climb SW on a path. Alternatively, for **Stage 6**, TL and go through the gate.

6 3:50: TL at a junction and cross the stream. Then continue climbing alongside the stream.

5 4:35: At a junction (rock with signs on it), keep SH. Soon the path climbs NW. Pass some beautiful lakes.

4 5:45: Climb a steep, loose path to reach **Col du Bastillon (2754m)**. On the W side of the col, a narrow path heads along the sheer edge of a slope: take care as the drops are steep. The route gradually bends left and eventually descends SW (red/white waymarks).

3 6:25: TL at a junction and head S. Soon reach the W tip of the largest of the **Lacs de Fenêtre**: continue S, passing between the next two lakes. Then climb S.

2 7:05: Keep SH across **Fenêtre de Ferret (2695m)**, entering **Italy**. Descend S on path 13A.

1 7:25: From the parking area beside **Alpeggio lo Baou** (farm shop and café), cross the road. Then head E on path 13A.

2 7:30: Keep SH at a junction and soon climb on the old cobbled pilgrims' path. Keep SH across the road: take great care as vehicles travel fast round the blind corner. Then climb a path through rock to a **statue of St-Bernard** near the restaurants on the Italian side of Col du GSB. Follow waymarks N up through rocks to cross the **Italy/Switzerland border**. The path then heads E just above the road: this is the old pilgrims' path to the col.

S 8:00: 5min later, reach the **monastery** at **Col du GSB (2469m)**.

Sunset at Col de Mille (Stage 1/v1/2a)

We thought guidebooks were boring so we decided to change them. Mapping is better than 40 years ago. Graphics are better than 40 years ago. Photography is better than 40 years ago. So why have walking guidebooks remained the same?

Well our guidebooks are **different**:

- **We use Real Maps.** You know, the **1:25,000/1:50,000** scale maps that walkers actually use to navigate with. Not sketch maps that get you lost. Real maps make more work for us but we think it is worth it. You do not need to carry separate maps and you are less likely to get lost so we save you time!
- **Numbered Waypoints** on our Real Maps link to the walk descriptions, making routes easier to follow than traditional text-based guidebooks. No more wading through pages of boring words to find out where you are! You want to look at incredible scenery and not have your face stuck in a book all day. Right?
- **Colour, colour, colour.** Mountains and cliffs are **beautiful** so guidebooks should be too. We were fed up using guidebooks which were ugly and boring. When planning, we want to be **dazzled** with full-size colour pictures of the **magnificence** which awaits us! So our guidebooks fill every inch of the page with beauty: big, **spectacular** photos of mountains, etc.
- **More practical size.** Long enough to have Real Maps and large pictures but slim enough to fit in a pocket.

Now all that sounds great to us but we want to know if you like what we have done. So hit us with your feedback: good or bad. We are not too proud to change.

Follow us for trekking advice, book updates, discount coupons, articles and other interesting hiking stuff.

 www.knifeedgeoutdoor.com

 info@knifeedgeoutdoor.com

 @knifeedgeoutdoor

 @knifeedgeout

 @knifeedgeoutdoor